EASY RUSSIAN
PHRASEBOOK & DICTIONARY

Ann Rolbin

PASSPORT BOOKS
NTC/Contemporary Publishing Company

Library of Congress Cataloging-in-Publication Data
is available from the United States Library of Congress.

Published by Passport Books
An imprint of NTC/Contemporary Publishing Company
4255 West Touhy Avenue, Lincolnwood (Chicago),
Illinois 60646-1975 U.S.A.
Copyright © 1995 by NTC Publishing Group
Manufactured in the United States of America
International Standard Book Number: 0-8442-4279-9

9   0   VP   9   8   7   6   5   4   3

Contents

Introduction

The Easy Russian Phrasebook and Dictionary will help you communicate in Russian and serve as a guide on your trip to Russia.

Every chapter includes contemporary expressions in English and Russian as well as phonetic transcriptions, travel tips, and culture notes. The appendices provide expressions of time, numbers, colors, days of the week, measurements, etc. In addition, there is an English-Russian/Russian-English vocabulary at the end of the book.

Russia and the Russian Language

On December 25, 1991 the Soviet Union was officially dissolved. The fifteen nations of the former Soviet Union are Russia, Belarus,Ukraine, Lithuania, Estonia, Latvia, Moldova, Georgia, Armenia, Azerbaijan, Turkmenistan, Uzbekistan, Kyrgyzstan, Kazakhstan, and Tajikistan. Nine of these nations are presently members of the Commonwealth of Independent States (CIS). These states are: Russia, Belarus, Ukraine, Armenia, Turkmenistan, Uzbekistan, Kyrgystan, Kazakhstan, and Tajikistan. Each of these nations has its own language, customs, and traditions.

The Russian language belongs to the Slavic language family. The Russian alphabet has thirty-three letters. Two other Slavic languages similar to Russian are spoken in Belarus and Ukraine.

Russian Alphabet and Pronunciation Guide

1. The Russian (Cyrillic) Alphabet

А	а	(a)	a as in *f*a*ther
Б	б	(b)	b as in *b*a*by
В	в	(v)	v as in *v*ictory
Г	г	(g)	g as in *g*arden
Д	д	(d)	d as in *d*a*d
Е	е	(ye)	ye as in *ye*s
Ё	ё	(yo)	yo as in *yo*ga
Ж	ж	(zh)	zh as in *Zh*a *Zh*a
З	з	(z)	z as in *z*oo
И	и	(i)	i as in mar*i*ne
Й	й	(y)	a short y-glide occurring after other vowels, like the y in bo*y*. To simplify transcription it is transcribed only when important for correct pronunciation.
К	к	(k)	k as in ma*k*e
Л	л	(l)	l as in ta*ll*
М	м	(m)	m as in *m*ap
Н	н	(n)	n as in *n*ever
О	о	(o)	o as in ph*o*ne
П	п	(p)	p as in *P*eter
Р	р	(r)	rolled like Spanish *r*
С	с	(s)	s as in *s*ad
Т	т	(t)	t as in *T*om
У	у	(u)	u as in fl*u*te
Ф	ф	(f)	f as in *f*ive
Х	х	(kh)	Like a heavily aspirated English *h*. Raise the tongue at the back of the mouth, in the position for *c* as in *c*ow, but say *h*ow.
Ч	ч	(ch)	ch as in *ch*eese
Ц	ц	(ts)	ts as in mel*ts*
Ш	ш	(sh)	sh as in *sh*ow
Щ	щ	(shch)	sh plus ch, like fre*sh ch*eese
Ъ	ъ	(hard sign)	No sound value. Separates letters.

Ы	ы	(y)	Similar to short i in English h*i*t but with the tongue higher. Say *hoot*, and, without moving your tongue, gradually relax your lips to the position they would be in for *hit*. The *y* used to transcribe this vowel should not be confused with the *y* that is part of vowels *ye, yo, yu,* or *ya,* or the *y* used after other vowels (bo*y*).
Ь	ь	(soft sign)	makes preceding consonant soft. Transliterated using apostrophe: пить (drink) = pit'
Э	э	(e)	e as in m*e*t
Ю	ю	(yu)	yu as in *yu*le
Я	я	(ya)	ya as in *ya*cht

2. Pronunciation Tips

While the Russian alphabet portrays the spoken language quite well, it is not as phonetic a representation as, for example, the Spanish alphabet. The following notes will help you pronounce Russian. The phonetic transcription incorporates the following guidelines and should help you pronounce accurately.

Consonants at the end of Russian words are pronounced unvoiced, i.e., a *v* sound is pronounced *f*, a *g* sound is pronounced *k*, etc. Devoicing also occurs when voiced consonants occur together with unvoiced consonants, e.g., вторник (Tuesday) is pronounced *ftórnik.*

Stress, or accent, in Russian words can fall on any syllable. Since it is completely arbitrary, it is marked throughout in the phonetic transcriptions. It is important to pay attention to where the stress falls, because it can make a difference in meaning. Example: му́ка means *torment,* but мука́ means *flour.*

Unstressed *o* is pronounced like a short *a* and is indicated as such in the transcriptions.

The vowel я (ya) loses its full quality when it occurs in unstressed syllables. It is pronounced like yi as in *yi*p. This is indicated in the phonetic transcriptions as *yi.* Be careful to distinguish between the *i* in this context and the full *i* sound (like b*ee*t), spelled by the letter и. Unstressed e (ye) is pronounced similarly in certain instances.

Silent letters occur in Russian only in some isolated words, such as the first **в** *(v)* in здравствуйте (zdrástvuytye). These are not shown in the phonetic transcriptions.

In reality, the Russian sound system is more complex than represented here. The *y*-glide before vowels, or quality of "softness", actually belongs to the soft consonant preceding a vowel. Some consonants are hard and are never followed by the *y*-glide. To be sure of your pronunciation always consult the transcriptions.

The short prepositions **в** *(v)*, **к** *(k)*, and **с** *(s)* are pronounced as part of the following word. *v* is pronounced *f* when followed by a voiceless consonant.

3. Gender

Russian nouns can be masculine (**m**), feminine (**f**), or neuter (**n**). In general, nouns ending in a consonant are masculine, nouns ending in *-a* are feminine, and nouns ending in *-o* are neuter. Nouns ending in –**ь** (') (the soft sign) can be masculine or feminine.

Past tense verb forms agree in gender and number with the speaker, with most masculine forms ending in *-l*, feminine forms in *-la,* and plural forms in *-li.*

When two or more forms of the same word are given (i.e. of different gender), they are separated by a slash.

The Basics

добро пожаловать!

Some knowledge of Russian will make your trip more enjoyable. You will be able to speak with the people, read signs, ask simple questions in your hotel, order food in restaurants, and much, much more. Your efforts to speak the language will be appreciated by all the Russians you meet.

Meeting and Greeting

Hello.	Zdrástvuitye.
Good morning.	Dóbraye útra.
Good afternoon.	Dóbry dyen'.
Good evening.	Dóbry vyéchyir.
How are you? (*formal*)	Kak pazhiváyitye?
And you?	A vy?
How are things? (*informal*)	Kak dyelá?
Thank you. I'm fine.	Spasíba kharashó.
How about you?	A u vas?
Welcome!	Dabró pazhálavat'!
I'm an American.	Ya amyerikányets (m.).
	Ya amyerikánka (f.).
My name is Victor.	Minyá zavút Víktar.
What is your name?	Kak vas zavút?
Where are you from?	Atkúda vy?
I'm from . .	Ya iz . . .
I'm glad to meet you.	Rat (m.)/ráda (f.) paznakómitsa.

Requests

Can you please tell me . . .	Skazhýtye, pazhálusta . . .
How do you get to . . . ?	Kak praytí . . . ?

Are they friendly?

Т
И
Р
S

Visitors to Russia often have the impression that Russians are unfriendly. People don't smile or make eye contact on the street or in stores, and they don't say "hello" to strangers. But foreigners who get to know Russians personally discover that they are warm and hospitable. They invite strangers to visit them at home and go out of their way to entertain them.

Key Words

Здравствуйте.

Доброе утро.

Добрый день.

Добрый вечер.

Как поживаете?

А вы?

Как дела?

Спасибо хорошо.

А у вас?

Добро пожаловать!

Я американец.

Я американка.

Меня зовут Виктор.

Как вас зовут?

Откуда вы?

Я из . . .

Рад/рада
познакомиться.

Скажите,
пожалуйста . . .

Как пройти . . . ?

Day and Date

today	sivódnya	сегодня
tomorrow	záftra	завтра
yesterday	fchyerá	вчера
morning	útra	утро
noon	póldyen	полдень
evening	vyéchir	вечер
night	noch	ночь
three days ago	tri dnya nazát	три дня назад
the day before yesterday	pozafcherá	позавчера
the day after tomorrow	poslyezáftra	послезавтра
three days from today	chyéris tri dnya	через три дня

Is it easy to ask directions?

Russians show a great interest in foreigners. If a foreigner has a question or needs directions, they will try their best to help and to make themselves clear.

Although foreign languages are required in Russian public schools and English is the most popular foreign language, very few high-school graduates are able to communicate easily with an English-speaking person.

Where is the restroom?	Gdye tualyét?
Can you please help me?	Pamagítye, pazhálusta.
Speak slowly, please.	Gavarítye myédlyinna, pazhálusta.
Please repeat.	Paftarítye, pazhálusta.
I don't understand.	Ya nyi panimáyu.
May I come in?	Razryeshítye vaytí.
Could you pass me the salad, please?	Piryidáytye, pazhálusta, salát.
Taxi!	Taksí!
Please take me to the museum, theater, airport . . .	Atvyizítye minyá, pazhálusta, vmuzyéy, ftyátr, vaerapórt . . .
Please stop at . . .	Astanavítyes', pazhálusta, u . . .

Expressing Thanks

Thank you.	Spasíba.
Thank you very much.	Bal'shóye spasíba.
Thank you for your gift, invitation, help, hospitality.	Spasíba za padárak, priglashéniye, pómashch, gastyepriímstva.
Thank you, it was delicious.	Spasíba, býla fkúsna.
Thank you for all you have done.	Spasíba za fsyo, shto vy dly minyá zdyélali.
You're welcome.	Pazhálusta.
You're very kind.	Vy óchin' dabrí.

Где туалет?

Помогите, пожалуйста.

Говорите медленно, пожалуйста.

Повторите, пожалуйста.

Я не понимаю.

Разрешите войти.

Передайте, пожалуйста, салат.

Такси!

Отвезите меня, пожалуйста, в музей, в театр, в аэропорт . . .

Остановитесь, пожалуйста, у . . .

Спасибо.

Большое спасибо.

Спасибо за подарок, приглашение, помощь, гостеприимство.

Спасибо, было вкусно.

Спасибо за всё, что вы для меня сделали.

Пожалуйста.

Вы очень добры.

Key words

smoke (v.)	kurít'	курить
men's room	muzhskóy tualyét	мужской туалет
ladies' room	zhénskiy tualyét	женский туалет
store	magazín	магазин
clothes	adyéshda	одежда
book	kníga	книга
umbrella	zont	зонт
east	vastók	восток
west	zápat	запад
south	yuk	юг
north	syévyer	север
on the left	slyéva	слева
to the left	na lyéva	налево
on the right	správa	справа
to the right	na práva	направо
rain	dózht'	дождь
snow	snyek	снег
humid	vlázhna	влажно

Polite Remarks

Congratulations!	Pazdravlyáyu!
Congratulations on your promotion!	Pazdravlyáyu spovyshéniyem!
Happy birthday!	Sdnyóm razhdyéniya!
I would like to introduce you to Mr. Petrov.	Paznakómtyes pazhálsta. Eta gaspadín Pyetróv.
Sit down, please.	Sadítyes pazhálusta.
Can I help?	Razrishítye pamóch?
I hope you will have a good time in Russia.	Nadyéyus vy kharashó pravidyóte vryémya fMaskvyé.

Questions

May I have your first and last name, please?	Vashe ímya i famíliya, pazhálusta?
Where is—the hotel, subway station, department store, post office, bus stop?	Gdye - gastínitsa, mitró, magazín, póchta, astanófka-aftóbusa?
How do I get to the Hotel Metropol, to . . . ?	Kak praytí k gastínitsye Myetrapól, K . . . ?
Where can I buy souvenirs?	Gdye mózhna kupít' suviníry?
Do you have—any nesting dolls, amber . . . ?	U vas yest' matryóshki, yantár . . . ?
What color, size, . . . ?	Kakóy tsvyet, razmyér . . . ?
How much is it?	Skól'ka stóit?
What time is it?	Skol'ka vryémini?
How do you say . . . ?	Kak skazát' . . . ?
Speak slowly, please.	Gavarítye myédlina, pazhalsta.
Please repeat.	Pavtarítye, pazhálusta.
Where can I get a taxi?	Gdye mózhna vzyat' taksí?
Do you like the food, the city . . . ?	Vam nrávitsa yedá, górat?
Are you open on Sunday?	Vy rabótayitye v vaskrisyénye?

Поздравляю!

Поздравляю с повышением!

С днем рождения!

Познакомьтесь, пожалуйста.
Это господин Петров.

Садитесь, пожалуйста.

Разрешите помочь?

Надеюсь, вы хорошо
проведёте время в Москве.

Ваше имя, фамилия,
пожалуйста.

Где – гостиница, метро,
магазин, почта, остановка
автобуса?

Как пройти к гостинице
Метрополь, к . . . ?

Где можно купить сувениры?

У вас есть матрёшки, янтарь
. . . ?

Какой цвет, размер . . . ?

Сколько стоит?

Сколько времени?

Как сказать?

Говорите медленно,
пожалуйста.

Повторите, пожалуйста.

Где можно взять такси?

Вам нравится еда, город?

Вы работаете в воскресенье?

| When does the bank, restaurant open, close? | Kagdá atkriváyitsa, zakryvayitsa bank, ristarán? |

Exclamations

Hurry up!	Bystrýey!
Very good!	Kharashó!
Excellent!	Atlíchna!
Wonderful!	Zamichátyel'na!
My God!	Góspadi!
That's too bad!	Ochin' zhal'!
What a beautiful day!	Kakóy kharóshiy dyen'!
Look out!	Astarózhna!
What a pity!	Kak zhal'!
I'm here!	Ya zdyes'!
Of course!	Kanyéshna!
What's wrong?	Shto sluchílas'?
Never mind!	Nichivó!
Ouch!	Oy!
Quiet, please!	Tíshye, pazhálusta!
Get out!	Výdi von!
Stop it!	Piristán'!
Good luck!	Fsyevó kharóshiva!
Bless you!	But' zdaróf (m.)/zdaróva (f.).
Cheers!	Nazdaróvye!

On the phone

| Hello! | Alyó |
| May I speak to Mr. Ivanov, please? | Paprasítye, pazhálusta gaspadína Ivanóva. |

Когда открывается,
закрывается банк, ресторан?

Быстрее!

Хорошо!

Отлично!

Замечательно!

Господи!

Очень жаль!

Какой хороший день!

Осторожно!

Как жаль!

Я здесь!

Конечно!

Что случилось?

Ничего.

Ой!

Тише, пожалуйста!

Выйди вон!

Перестань!

Всего хорошего!

Будь здоров/здорова!

На здоровье!

Алло

Попросите, пожалуйста,
господина Иванова.

Speaking!	Eta ya. Ya slúshayu!
Whom do you want to speak to?	Skyem vy khatítye gavarít'?
He's not home.	Yevó nyet dóma.
Do you want to leave a message for him?	Vy khotítye yemú shto nibút' piridát'?
Please tell him that I called.	Piridáytye, pazhálusta, shto ya zvaníl.
I'll tell him.	Ya yemú piridám.
I'll call back later.	Ya piryezvanyú pózhe.
You've got the wrong number.	Vy ni tudá papáli.
How do I make a long-distance call to America?	Kak mnye pazvanít' vamyériku?
How long do I have to wait?	Skól'ka vryémyeni mnye núzhna zhdat'?
The line is busy.	Zányita.

Apologies

| Excuse me. | Izvinítye. |
| I apologize. | Prashú proshchéniya. |

On the phone

Т
П
Р
С

In major cities, most people have telephones in their homes. In small towns and remote villages, however, telephones are still rare. Telephone numbers in Moscow, St. Petersburg, and Kiev have seven digits, while numbers in other cities have six. There are places that you can contact by dialing direct, but you usually have to ask the operator for assistance. You can also buy a coupon for long-distance calls at the local post office or telephone company. You pay for the number of minutes you wish to speak on the phone.

When people answer the phone, they usually say "Alyo."

Это я.
Я слушаю!

С кем вы хотите говорить?

Его нет дома.

Вы хотите ему что–нибудь
передать?

Передайте, пожалуйста, что я
звонил.

Я ему передам.

Я перезвоню.

Вы не туда попали.

Как мне позвонить в
Америку?

Сколько времени мне нужно
ждать?

Занято.

Извините.

Прошу прощения.

Russian names

The most common Russian names for men are Ivan, Mikhail (diminutive: Misha), Boris (diminutive: Borya). The most common women's names are Natasha, Tanya, and Marina.

Pardon me.	Prastítye.
I wasn't intending to . . .	Ya ni sabirálsya . . .
I'm sorry.	Vinavát (m.)/vinaváta (f.).
I'm sorry, but I can't help you.	Ksazhilyéniyu, ya ni magú vam pamóch.
That's all right.	Nichivó.

Help

Help!	Pamagítye! Karaúl!
Call the police!	Pazvanítye v milítsiyu!
Call a doctor!	Výzavitye vrachá!
Call an ambulance!	Výzavitye skóruyu pómashch.
Take me back to my hotel please.	Atvizítye, pazhálsta, minyá abrátna vgastínitsu.
Fire!	Pazhár!
He was in a car accident.	On papál vaftamabíl'nuyu aváriyu.
He was hit by a car.	On papál pad mashínu.

Good-byes

Good-bye!	Da svidániya!
Have a good trip!	Shchislívava putí!
See you later.	Da skórava. paká.
I'm afraid I must go now.	Ksazhilýeniyu, mnye pará ittí.
Take good care of yourself.	Birigí syebyá, but' zdaróf.
I hope to see you again.	Nadyéyus', ya vas yishchó uvízhu.
Please come again if you have a chance.	Yésli u vas búdyet vozmózhnast', prikhadítye, pazhálusta.
Write to us if you have time.	Napishítye nam, yésli u vas budyet vryémya.
Please say hello for me to your wife, sister, husband	Piridáytye, pazhálusta, privyét váshiy zhinyé, sistryé, múzhu . . .

Простите.

Я не собирался . . .

Виноват, виновата.

К сожалению, я не могу вам помочь.

Ничего.

Помогите! Караул!

Позвоните в милицию!

Вызовите врача!

Вызовите скорую помощь.

Отвезите меня, пожалуйста, обратно в гостиницу.

Пожар!

Он попал в автомобильную аварию.

Он попал под машину.

До свидания!

Счастливого пути!

До скорого, пока.

К сожалению, мне пора идти.

Береги себя, будь здоров.

Надеюсь, я вас еще увижу.

Если у вас будет возможность, приходите, пожалуйста.

Напишите нам, если у вас будет время.

Передайте, пожалуйста, привет вашей жене, сестре, мужу . . .

Countries and Peoples

United States	Sayedinyónyye Shtáty
America	Amyérika
American	Amyerikanyets (m.)
	Amyerikánka (f.)
Russia	Rassíya
Russian	Rússkiy (m.)
	Rússkaya (f.)
France	Frántsiya
Frenchman	Frantsús
Frenchwoman	Frantsúzhinka
England	Angliya
Englishman	Anglichánin
Englishwoman	Anglichánka
Canada	Kanáda
Canadian	Kanádyets (m.)
	Kanátka (f.)
Italy	Itáliya
Italian	Ital'yányets (m.)
	Ital'yánka (f.)
Spain	Ispániya
Spaniard	Ispányets (m.)
	Ispánka (f.)

What You May Hear

Zdrástvuytye!	Hello!
Spasíba.	Thank you.
Kharashó.	OK, good.
Padazhdítye minútku.	Wait a second.
Zakhadítye pazhálusta.	Please come in.
Sadítyes', pazhálusta.	Take a seat please.

Соединенные Штаты

Америка

Американец
Американка

Россия

Русский
Русская

Франция

Француз

Француженка

Англия

Англичанин

Англичанка

Канада

Канадец
Канадка

Италия

Итальянец
Итальянка

Испания

Испанец
Испанка

Здравствуйте!

Спасибо.

Хорошо.

Подождите минутку.

Заходите, пожалуйста.

Садитесь, пожалуйста.

Travel

The two most common means of travel in Russia are by air or by train. All trains have sleeping and dining cars. During the summer, Russians like to travel to resorts located along the major rivers and on the Black Sea. Business people and tourists take advantage of the overnight trains, the *Strela (Red Arrow),* from Moscow to St. Petersburg and from Moscow to Kiev. Travelers from abroad have to pay for their tickets in dollars, marks, yen, francs, or other hard currencies.

The ruble is the official Russian currency. You can exchange American dollars for Russian rubles in hotels, foreign exchange offices, and banks. Private exchange is illegal.

At Customs

May I have your passport and customs declaration form?	Paśpart i tamózhinuyu diklarátsiyu, pazhálusta.
What is the purpose of your trip?	Kakáya tsel' váshy payéstki?
Tourism.	Turízm.
This is my first time in Russia.	Ya pyérvy ras v Rassíí.
This is my passport.	Vot moy páspart.
There are five of us in a group.	Vgrúppe pyat' chilavýek.
This painting is a gift from one of my Russian friends.	Éta kartína padárak mayivó rússkava druga.
I was told that I could take this box.	Mnye skazáli shto etu shkatúlku mózhna vzyat' ssabóy.
This is the receipt.	Vot chek.
Anything else?	Shto nibút' yishchó?
I have lost my passport.	Ya patirýal (m.)/patirýala (f.) páspart.
I have a favor to ask of you.	U minýa kvam bal'sháya prós'ba.
May I phone my embassy?	Mózhna pazvanít' v pasól'stva?

Passports and Money

𝕋
𝕀
ℙ
𝕊

At the age of 16 every Russian citizen receives a passport. Russians do not have Social Security numbers, so a passport is the major identification document containing a person's vital information: date and place of birth, address, and nationality.

The ruble is the basic monetary unit in Russia. Until the beginning of the nineties, ruble notes came in denominations of one, three, five, ten, fifty, and one hundred rubles. Due to inflation, the government later introduced new notes in denominations of 500, 1000, 5000, 10,000, and 50,000 rubles.

Key Words

Паспорт и таможенную декларацию пожалуйста.

Какая цель вашей поездки?

Туризм.

Я первый раз в России.

Вот мой паспорт.

В группе пять человек.

Эта картина подарок моего русского друга.

Мне сказали, что эту шкатулку можно взять с собой.

Вот чек.

Что–нибудь ещё?

Я потеряла паспорт.

У меня к вам большая просьба.

Можно позвонить в посольство?

passport	páspart	паспорт
customs	tamózhnya	таможня
declaration form	diklarátsiya	декларация
foreign currency	valyúta	валюта
jewelry	dragatsénnasti	драгоценности
painting	kartína	картина
antique	starínny	старинный
medicine	likárastva	лекарство
pen	atkrýt	открыт
closed	zakrýt	закрыт
suitcase	chimadán	чемодан
luggage	bagázh	багаж
bank	bánk	банк
exchange	abmyén	обмен
U.S. dollar	amyerikánskiy dóllar	американский доллар
British Sterling	anglískiy styérlink	английский стерлинг
Japanese Yen	yipónskaya yéna	японская йена
Deutsche Mark	nimyétskaya márka	немецкая марка

"We'll Pay Cash."

Cash is almost the only means of carrying out financial transactions in Russia. Checks, though in existence, are rarely used for purchases. Large sums of money are kept in banks (*sberegatelnaya kassa*), though the interest is low. To pay for purchases, people usually withdraw money from the bank.

Money in Russia

Do you accept American dollars?	Vy prinimáyitye amyerikánskiye dóllary?
Where can I exchange U.S. dollars?	Gdye mózhna paminyát' dóllary?
What time does the exchange open?	Kagdá atkryváyitsa abmýeny punkt?
Can I change money in the hotel?	Mózhna abminyát' dyén'gi vgastínitsye?
I want to exchange U.S. dollars for rubles.	Ya khochú abminyát' amyerikánskiye dóllary na rublí.
What is today's exchange rate?	Kakóy sivódnya abmýény kurs?
Please give it to me in large bills.	Dáytye, pazhálusta, fkrúpnykh banknótakh.
I want to change rubles for U.S. dollars.	Ya khachú paminyát' rublí na dóllary.
Here is my receipt.	Vot mayá kvitántsiyu.

Booking a Plane Ticket

Can I go by plane to Kiev?	Mózhna palityét' v Kíyev na samalýotye?
What time is my flight?	Va skol'ka ya ulitáyu?

Major cities of the Commonwealth of Independent States (CIS) are served by many international airlines. Among the airlines are: Air France, Lufthansa, Swiss Air, British Airways, Delta, Japan Airlines, Czech Air, Finn Air, Air China, Iberia, and Canadian International. Flights between cities in Russia or in the former republics are handled by Aeroflot. Remember that delays at the airport are very common.

Key Words

Вы принимаете американские доллары?	receipt	kvitántsiya	квитанция
	credit card	kridítnaya kártachka	кредитная карточка
Где можно обменять доллары?	take off	vylitát'	вылетать
	landing	prizimlýatsa	приземляться
Когда открывается обменный пункт?	arrival	pribýtiye	прибытие
	flight	ryéys, palýot	рейс, полёт
Можно обменять деньги в гостинице?	plane	samalýot	самолет
Я хочу обменять американские доллары на рубли.	airport	aerapórt	аэропорт
	plane ticket	bilyét na samalýot	билет на самолет
Какой сегодня обменный курс?	seat	myésta, sidýeniye	место, сидение
Дайте, пожалуйста, в крупных банкнотах.	weather	pagóda	погода
	temperature	timpyeratúra	температура
Я хочу поменять рубли на доллары.	information office	správachnaye byuró	справочное бюро
Вот моя квитанция.	luggage	bagázh	багаж
	luggage claim	kvitántsiya na bagázh	квитанция на багаж
Можно полететь в Киев на самолёте?	check the luggage	zdat' bagázh	сдать багаж

Во сколько я улетаю?

Т
П
Р
S

Trains are the most common means of transportation between cities in the CIS. Passenger trains have several classes: first class or international has soft seats which become beds and the compartments are for two people. The class below has benches which also serve as beds and the compartments are for four. Every train has a dining car. Travel by train gives the tourist an opportunity to see the countryside and meet the people.

There are several train stations in the major cities. Remember that it is very important to know the name of the station from which your train departs.

Where can I buy a plane ticket?	Gdye mózhna kupít' bilyét na samalyot?
How much is the ticket?	Skól'ka stóit bilyet?
I need two tickets.	Mnye núzhna dva bilyéta.
When should I be at the airport?	Kagdá mnye núzhna byt' vaerapartú?
How long does it take to get to the airport?	Za skól'ka vrýemini my dayédyem da aerapartá?

Planes

How long is the flight to Kiev?	Skól'ka vrýemini litýet' da Kíyeva?
When will we arrive in Minsk?	Kagdá my prilitím vMinsk?
Is it cold, warm, hot in Tbilisi?	FTbilísi khóladna, tipló, zhárka?
Where can I check my luggage?	Gdye zdayút bagázh?
Where can I pick up my luggage?	Gdye palucháyut bagázh?
This is my luggage claim.	Vot mayá bagázhnaya kvitántsiya.
When will Flight No. . . . take off?	Kagdá vylitáyet samalyót rýeysa . . . ?

СЖД	АСУ «ЭКСПРЕСС»	ПРОЕЗДНОЙ ДОКУМЕНТ		ТБ	612721

Где можно купить
билет на самолёт?

Сколько стоит
билет?

Мне нужно два
билета.

Когда мне нужно
быть в аэропорту?

За сколько времени
мы доедем до
аэропорта?

Сколько времени
лететь до Киева?

Когда мы прилетим
в Минск?

В Тбилиси холодно,
тепло, жарко?

Где сдают багаж?

Где получают
багаж?

Вот моя багажная
квитанция.

Когда вылетает
самолёт рейса . . . ?

Key Words

how much does . . . cost?	skól'ka stóit . . . ?	сколько стоит . . . ?
railway station	zhilyéznada-rózhnaya stántsiya	железнод-орожная станция
train	póyist	поезд
train ticket	bilyét na póyist	билет на поезд
platform	platfórma	платформа

How do I call Aeroflot?	Kak pazvanít' vAeraflót?
I would like to confirm my reservation.	Ya khachú patvirdít' moy ryéys.
Is this a direct flight?	Éta primóy rýeys?
Where are we now?	Gdye my sichás litím?
Please bring me a cup of ice water.	Prinisítye, pazhálusta, stakán vadý sal'dóm.

Trains

How do I get to the train station?	Kak dayékhat' da vakzála?
Where do I buy train tickets?	Gdye pradayústsa bilyéty na póyist?
How much is a train ticket?	Skól'ka stóit bilyét na póyist?
When is the next train?	Kagdá atkhódit slyédushchiy póyist?
How long will the train wait at this station?	Skól'ka vryémini póyist staít na étay stántsii?
Can I have (this) ticket changed for tomorrow?	Mózhna paminyát' bilyét na zaftra?
Is there a dining car on this train?	Vétam póyizdye yest' vagón-ristarán?
How many people are in one compartment?	Skól'ka chyelovýek vadnóm kupé?
How long does it take to get from Moscow to . . . ?	Skól'ka vrýemini yékhat' at Maskvý da . . . ?
When does the train arrive in . . . ?	Kagdá póyist pribyváyit v . . . ?
This train departs from . . . train station.	État póyist atpravlýayitsa s . . . vakzála.

What You May Hear

| Vnimánye pasazhíri! | Attention passengers! |
| Pred'yavíte, pazhálusta: páspart | Please show your: passport |

Как позвонить в Аэрофлот?

Я хочу подтвердить мой рейс.

Это прямой рейс?

Где мы сейчас летим?

Принесите, пожалуйста, стакан
воды со льдом.

Как доехать до вокзала?

Где продаются билеты на поезд?

Сколько стоит билет на поезд?

Когда отходит следующий поезд?

Сколько времени поезд стоит на
этой станции?

Можно поменять билет на завтра?

В этом поезде есть вагон–ресторан?

Сколько человек в одном купе?

Сколько времени ехать от Москвы
до . . . ?

Когда поезд прибывает в . . . ?

Этот поезд отправляется с . . .
вокзала.

Внимание пассажиры!

Предъявите, пожалуйста:
паспорт

diklarátsiyu	declaration form
bagázhnuyu kvitántsiyu	baggage claim
My príbyli v . . .	We have arrived in . . .
Ryéys nómer . . . apázdivayet	Flight # . . . is late.
VMaskvyé khóladna	It is cold in Moscow.
Kudá vy idyótye?	Where are you going?
Vam núzhna taksi?	Need a taxi?
Idítye za mnoy, pazhálusta	Follow me, please.

декларацию
багажную квитанцию

Мы прибыли в . . .

Рейс номер . . . опаздывает

в Москве холодно.

Вам нужно такси?
Идите за мной, пожалуйста.

Health care in Russia and the other former Soviet republics is free. However, there are also private doctors, dentists, labs, and small hospitals. Small private hospitals offer treatment and diagnostic medicine. Doctors will usually make house calls when the patient is too sick to visit the office. Most doctors do not speak English.

Common cold medicines are available in drugstores without prescriptions. Other medications will require a prescription from a doctor.

Seeing a Doctor

Where is the doctor's office?	Gdye paliklínka?
Where is the hospital?	Gdye bal'nítsa?
Is there a doctor in the hotel?	Yest' li dóktar vgastínitsye?
Where is the drugstore?	Gdye aptýeka?
Can I buy some medicine in the hotel?	Mózhna kupít likárstva vgastínitsye?
I want to buy some medicine to cure . . .	Ya khachú kupít' likárstva at . . .
Can you accompany me to the doctor?	Vy ni maglí by paytí sa mnóy k vrachú?
Can a doctor make a house call?	Mózhna výzvat' vrachá nádam?
Do I need a prescription to buy this medicine?	Mnye núzhin ritsyépt shtóby kupít eta likárstva?

At the Doctor's Office

I have a sore throat.	U minyá balít górla.
I have a cough.	U minyá káshil'.

Seeing a doctor

The majority of the population takes advantage of the socialized system of health care, to which all citizens have access. On rare occasions, people go to private doctors, more often than not for a second opinion. Also, every primary-care physician is assigned to certain areas or neighborhoods, so people are not able to choose a physician unless they want to see a private doctor.

Primary-care physicians give referrals to specialists if necessary, but complete physicals and other types of preventive care are less common than in the West. Herbal treatments and physical therapy are very popular.

There is no medical insurance in Russia.

Key Words

Где поликлиника?	tests	análizy	анализы
Где больница?	penicillin	pyenitsíllin	пенициллин
Есть ли доктор в гостинице?	allergy	allergíya	аллергия
	reaction	riáktsiya	реакция
Где аптека?	side effect	pabóchnaye yivlyéniye	побочное явление
Можно купить лекарство в гостинице?	high blood pressure	vysókaye davlyéniye	высокое давление
	low blood pressure	niskaye davlyéniye	низкое давление
Я хочу купить лекарство от . . .	take medicine	prinimát' likárstva	принимать лекарство
Вы не могли бы пойти со мной к врачу?	operation	apirátsiya	операция
	doctor's office	paliklínka	поликлиника
Можно вызвать врача на дом?	hospital	bal'nítsa	больница
	arm	ruká	рука
Мне нужен рецепт, чтобы купить это лекарство?	leg	nagá	нога
	head	galavá	голова
	heart	syértsye	сердце
	back	spiná	спина
	ear	úkha	ухо
У меня болит горло.	eye	glas	глаз
У меня кашель.	mouth	rot	рот

How many sick days?

T
I
P
S

Russians do not have a specific number of sick days that they can take off from work. If a person is sick enough to stay home from work, he or she has to get a certificate from a doctor.

Dentists, like primary-care physicians, are assigned to certain neighborhoods, and there are private dentists and dental clinics as well.

I have a fever.	U minyá timpyiratúra.
I have a headache.	U minyá bolít galavá.
I feel dizzy.	U minyá krúzhitsa galavá.
I feel like vomiting.	Minyá tashnít.
There is no pain there.	Zdyés ni bolít.
You probably have a cold.	Navyérna, vy prastudílis'.
Please prescribe me some medicine.	Výpishitye pazhálusta, mnye likárstva.
I feel pain here.	Vot zdyes' balít.
When will I feel better?	Kagdá ya búdu lúchshe sibyá chústvavat'?
Do I need an operation?	Mnye nuzhná apirátsiya?
Is it serious?	Éta sir'yózna?
Should I stay home or I can go out?	Mnye núzhna sidét' dóma ili mózhna vykhadít'?

At the drugstore

You cannot buy medications in supermarkets or grocery stores. Medications are available only in drugstores. A drugstore is called an "apteka."

Pharmacies in Russia do not sell anything other than medication, unlike drugstores in the United States. Drugstores carry only prescription and nonprescription medications and light medical supplies for home use, such as thermometers, hot pads, etc.

There are usually no drugstores or gift shops in Russian hospitals.

У меня температура.

У меня болит голова.

У меня кружится голова.

Меня тошнит.

Здесь не болит.

Наверно, вы простудились.

Выпишите, пожалуйста, мне лекарство.

Вот здесь болит.

Когда я буду лучше себя чувствовать?

Мне нужна операция?

Это серьезно?

Мне нужно сидеть дома или можно выходить?

Key Words

knee	kalyéna	колено
neck	shéya	шея
abdomen	zhivót	живот
stomach	zhilúdak	желудок
face	litsó	лицо
hip	bidró	бедро
finger	pályets	палец
a broken bone	pirilóm	перелом
a head cold	násmark	насморк
a cold	prastúda	простуда
a headache	galavnáya bol'	головная боль
a toothache	zubnáya bol'	зубная боль
a stomach ache	bolít zhilúdak	болит желудок
food poisoning	pishchivóye atravlyéniye	пищевое отравление
a swelling, tumor	ópukhal'	опухоль
sunstroke	sólnichniy udár	солнечный удар
sunburn	sólnichniy azhók	солнечный ожог
a heart attack	sirdyéchniy prístup	сердечный приступ

How many days should I stay home?	Skól'ka dnyey mnye nil'zyá vykhadít' iz dóma?
I feel better.	Ya lúchshe sibýa chústvuyu.
When should I come back?	Kagdá mnye núzhna prití fslýedushchiy ras?
I am allergic to . . .	U minyá allirgíya na . . . .
May I ask you to use a disposable needle?	Ya khachú paprasít' vas pól'zavatsa adnarázavoy iglóy.

At the Dentist

I have a toothache.	U minyá balít zup.
On the right, left.	Správa, slyéva
I hope it is not serious.	Nadýeyus', nichyevó sir'yóznava.
I need a filling.	Mnye nuzhná plómba.
I think I have broken a tooth.	Mnye kázhitsa, u minyá slamálsya zup.
Will you pull the tooth?	Vy búdyetye udalyát' zup?
Will you numb the tooth?	Vy zdyélayitye zamarósku?

At the Drugstore

I need to have the prescription filled.	Mnye núzhna zakazát' likárstva.
Is this medicine in tablets?	Eta likárstva ftablyétkakh?
When will the medicine be ready?	Kagdá likárstva búdyet gatóva?

Сколько дней мне нельзя выходить из дома?		

Я лучше себя чувствую.

Когда мне нужно прийти в следующий раз?

У меня аллергия на . . . .

Я хочу попросить вас пользоваться одноразовой иглой.

У меня болит зуб.

Справа, слева.

Надеюсь, ничего серьезного.

Мне нужна пломба.

Мне кажется, у меня сломался зуб.

Вы будете удалять зуб?

Вы сделаете заморозку?

Мне нужно заказать лекарство.

Это лекарство в таблетках?

Когда лекарство будет готово?

Key Words

sore throat	angína	ангина
strep throat	striptakók-kavaya angína	стрептокок-ковая ангина
right/left ear hurts	balít právaye/ lyévaye úkha	болит правое/левое ухо
right/left eye hurts	balít práviy/ lyéviy glas	болит правый/ левый глаз
a fever	timpiratúra, zhar	температура, жар
a cough	káshil'	кашель
diarrhea	panós	понос
an upset stomach	rasstróystva zhilútka	расстройство желудка
constipation	zapór	запор
a bruise	ushýp	ушиб
a doctor (M.D.)	vrach, dóktar	врач, доктор
a dentist	zubnóy vrach	зубной врач

How many times a day should I take this medicine?	Skól'ka ras vdyen' núzhna prinimat' likárstva?
How many pills?	Skól'ka tablyétak?
I am already taking medicine	Ya uzhé prinimáyu likárstva . . . .
May I take . . . and . . . together?	Mózhna prinimát' . . . i . . . vmyéstye?
Should I take this medicine before or after meals?	Eta likárstva núzhna prinimát' do yedý ili pósli yedý?
Please give me something for an upset stomach. a headache, heartburn, a cough, a cold.	Dáyte, pazhálusta, shtó-nibut' at rasstróystva zhilútka, galavnóy bóli, izzhógi, káshlya, prastúdi.
May I get this medicine without a prescription?	Mózhna kupít éta likárstva bes ritsépta?

What You May Hear

Pamyértye timpiratúru!	Take your temperature!
Atkróitye rot!	Open your mouth!
Zdyés' balít?	Does it hurt?
Lazhítyes'!	Lie down!
Dyshítye!	Breathe!
Pakáshlitye!	Cough!
Ni valnúityes!	Take it easy.
Ritsépt	Prescription
Aptyéka	Drugstore
Prinimáitye likárstva	Take medicine
Vy skóra paprávityes'	You will feel better soon.

Сколько раз в день нужно
принимать лекарство?

Сколько таблеток?

Я уже принимаю лекартсво
. . . .

Можно принимать . . . и . . .
вместе?

Это лекарство нужно
принимать до еды или после?

Дайте, пожалуйтса, что–
нибудь от расстройства
желудка, головной боли,
изжоги, кашля, простуды.

Можно купить это лекарство
без рецепта?

Померьте температуру!

Откройте рот!

Здесь болит?

Ложитесь!

Дышите!

Покашлейте!

Не волнуйтесь.

Рецепт

Аптека

Принимайте лекарство

Вы скоро поправитесь.

Transportation

You can travel within the cities by bus, trolley, streetcar, taxi, or subway. The subway is called the *Metro*.

Senior citizens use public transportation free of charge. Mass transit is crowded on weekdays between 4:30 P.M.— 7:00 P.M.

Buses, Trolleys, Street Cars

Excuse me. Which bus should I take to get to the Bolshoi Theatre?

Izvinítye. Na kakóm aftóbusye mózhna dayékhat' da Bal'shóva tiátra?

Where should I get off?

Gdye mnye vykhadít'?

How much is the bus fare?

Skól'ka stóit bilyét na aftóbus?

How many stops before the Bolshoi Theatre?

Skól'ka astanóvak da Bal'shóva tiátra?

Would you please tell me when I should get off?

Skazhítye, pazhálusta, gdye mnye vykhadít'?

Where is the bus, trolley stop?

Gdye astanófka aftóbusa, tralyéybusa?

Where should I transfer to bus number three?

Gdye mnye núzhna zdyélat' pirisátku na trétiy aftóbus?

Excuse me. Do you get off here?

Izviníte. Vy zdyes' vykhóditye?

Please let me by.

Razrishítye praytí.

Public transportation

Т
І
Р
Ѕ

Major cities, such as Moscow, St. Petersburg, and Kiev, have well-developed and very convenient subway systems—the metro. The metro is the fastest, safest, and most popular means of transportation. Trains come every one to two minutes during rush hours and every three to five minutes at night. Muscovites are especially proud of their metro. A ride on the Moscow metro is like a trip to a museum because of the system's unique engineering and architectural design. While most of the stations are deep underground, there are sections that are elevated. You will certainly enjoy riding the metro. Try to get off the train at several stations to look around.

Key Words

Извините. На каком
автобусе можно
доехать до Большого
театра?

Где мне выходить?

Сколько стоит билет
на автобус?

Сколько остановок
до Большого театра?

Скажите,
пожалуйста, где мне
выходить?

Где остановка
автобуса,
троллейбуса?

Где мне нужно
сделать пересадку на
третий автобус?

Извините. Вы злесь
выходите?

Разрешите пройти.

bus stop	aftóbusnaya astanófka	автобусная остановка
trolley stop	trallyébusnaya astanófka	троллейбусная остановка
bus number five	pyátiy aftóbus	пятый автобус
get on	fkhadít'	входить
get off	vykhadít'	выходить
transfer	dyelat' pirisátku	делать пересадку

You can either hail a taxi at designated places on the street, or call for
one by phone, which is more difficult. Available taxis usually have a
little green light in the front window.

Buses, streetcars, and trolleys are not as convenient as the metro.
People have to wait in long lines at bus stops. When you use public
transportation, keep in mind that you have to get up and head for the
door well before your stop. All forms of public transportation are very
crowded at rush hour. Passengers can purchase books of tickets for
use on any of the buses, trolleys, and streetcars, or they can pay their
fare during the ride.

Smaller towns usually have buses only. Some remote villages do
not have any public transportation at all, though there are buses or
local trains between villages.

Does this bus go to the . . . ?	État aftóbus idyót da . . . ?
How many stops before . . . ?	Skól'ka astanóvak da . . . ?
What is the next stop?	Kakáya slyédushchaya astanófka?
Which way is to . . . ?	Fkakúyu stóranu yékhat' da . . . ?

Subway

Where is the subway entrance?	Gdye fkhot vmitró?
Which way should I go?	Fkakúyu stóranu mnye núzhna yékhat'?
Does the subway go to . . . ?	Mózhna dayékhat' na mitró da . . . ?
How often do the subway trains run?	Kak chásta khódyat payizdá vmitró?
Where should I transfer to?	Gdye mnye núzhna zdyélat' pirisátku?
Is the exit at the next station on the left or on the right?	Na slyédushchiy stántsii výkhat správa ili slyéva?

Getting around

T
I
P
S

Traffic in big cities is heavy, and there are a lot of pedestrians on the streets during the day. Traffic rules are similar to those of the U.S. with a few differences. For example, there is no right turn on a red light.

It is often difficult to cross the street because of the number of cars and trucks on the road. Be very careful and remember to walk only on the sidewalk and to cross the street only at pedestrian crossings, which are sometimes underground tunnels. If you drive, do not exceed the city speed limit, which is 60 kilometers or 35 miles per hour. Even if you've had only one drink, don't drive.

Этот автобус идёт
до . . . ?

Сколько остановок
до . . . ?

Какая следующая
остановка?

В какую сторону
ехать до . . . ?

Где вход в метро?

В какую сторону
мне нужно ехать?

Можно доехать на
метро до . . . ?

Как часто ходят
поезда в метро?

Где мне нужно
сделать пересадку?

На следующей
станции выход
справа или слева?

Key Words

traffic light	svitafór	светофор
red light	krásniy svyet	красный свет
green light	zilyóniy svyet	зелёный свет
intersection	pirikryóstak	перекрёсток
buy a ticket	kupít' bilyét	купить билет
subway	mitró	метро
entrance	fkhot	вход
exit	výkhat	выход
direction	napravlyéniye	направление
time	vryémya	время
taxi	taksí	такси
driver	vadítyel'	водитель
fare	pláta za prayést	плата за проезд
wait	zhdat'	ждать
road	daróga	дорога
address	ádryes	адрес
street car	tramváy	трамвай

Taxi

Where can I get a taxi?	Gdye mózhna vzyát' taksí?
Where is the taxi stand?	Gdye stayánka taksí?
How much is it to . . . ?	Skól'ka stóit prayékhat' da . . . ?
Is this cab available?	Táksi svabódna?
I would like to go to . . .	Mnye núzhna dayékhat' da . . . .
Bolshoi Theatre, please.	Balshóy tiátr, pazhálusta.
Can you wait for me?	Vy ni maglí by padazhdát'?
I will be back in five minutes.	Ya pridú chyéris pyát' minút.
Please stop here for a moment.	Astanavítyes', pazhálusta, zdyes' na minútku.
Please take me to:	Atvizítye, pazhálusta v:
the hotel	gastínitsu.
the airport.	aerapórt.
the museum.	muzyéy.
How much do I owe you?	Skól'ka sminyá?

On Foot

I am going for a walk.	Ya idú pragulyátsa.
Is Red Square far from here?	Krásnaya plóshchad' dalikó atsyúda?
From here, turn right at the intersection and you will see it.	Atsyúda pavirnítye napráva na pirikryóstkye i vy uvíditye yeyó.
Could you tell me how to get there?	Vy ni skázhitye kak tudá praytí?

Где можно взять
такси?

Где стоянка такси?

Сколько стоит
проехать до . . . ?

Такси свободно?

Мне нужно доехать
до . . .

Большой театр,
пожалуйста.

Вы не могли бы
подождать?

Я приду через пять
минут.

Остановитесь,
пожалуйста, здесь на
минутку.

Отвезите,
пожалуйста, в –
гостиницу.
аэропорт.
музей.

Сколько с меня?

Я иду прогуляться.

Красная площадь
далеко отсюда?

Отсюда поверните
направо на
перекрёстке и вы
увидете её.

Вы не скажете как
туда пройти?

Key Words

take a walk	gulyát', praguly átsa	гулять, прогуляться
to the right	na práva	направо
to the left	na lyéva	налево
on the right	správa	справа
on the left	slyéva	слева
street	úlitsa	улица
alley	piriúlak	переулок
park	park	парк
hotel	gastínitsa	гостиница
theater	tyatr	театр
museum	muzyéy	музей
art gallery	kartínaya galiryéya	картинная галерея
restaurant	ristarán	ресторан
store	magazín	магазин
grocery store	pradavól'stveniy magazín	продовольс- твенный магазин
book store	knízhniy magazín	книжный магазин
men's room	mushskóy tualyét	мужской туалет
ladies' room	zhénskiy tualyét	женский туалет

Does this alley lead to the main street?	État piriúlak vykhódit na glávnuyu úlitsu?
What street is ahead?	Kakáya úlitsa fpiridí?
I am lost.	Ya patiryálsya.
Excuse me, where is Hotel . . . ?	Izvinítye, gdye gastínitsa . . . ?
Down the street and to the left.	Pryámo pa étoy úlitsye i nalýeva.
How long will it take me to get there?	Za skól'ka vryémini ya tudá daydú?
It takes about an hour to get there.	Tudá ittí ókala chásu.

What You May Hear

Kudá vy idyóte?	Where are you going?
Vy vikhódiyte?	Are you getting off?
Razrishítye praytí.	Let me pass please.
Mnyé núzhna pirisyést' na aftóbus A.	I need to transfer to bus A.
Slyédushchaya astanofka . . .	The next stop is . . .
Pakazhítye, pazhálusta, bilyét.	Show your ticket please.
Snachála dáytye lyúdyam výti patóm vy zaydyótye.	First, let people get off, then you get on.
Izvinítye.	Excuse me.
Piridáytye, pazhálusta, dén'gi za bilyét.	Please pass this money for a ticket.
Vam sichás vykhadít'.	You have to get off now.
Sadítyes', pazhálusta.	Please take a seat.
Spasíba, ya pastayú.	Thank you, I'll stand.
Skól'ka stóit bilyét?	How much is the ticket?
Ya patiryál bilyét.	I've lost my ticket.
Da tyátra ishchó tri astanófki.	There are three more stops till the theater.

Этот переулок выходит на
главную улицу?

Какая улица впереди?

Я потерялся.

Извините, где гостиница . . . ?

Прямо по этой улице и налево.

За сколько времени я туда
дойду?

Туда идти около часу.

Куда вы идёте?

Вы выходите?

Разрешите пройти.

Мне нужно пересесть на
автобус А.

Следующая остановка . . .

Покажите, пожалуйста,
билет.

Сначала дайте людям выйти,
потом вы зайдёте.

Извините.

Передайте, пожалуйста, деньги
за билет.

Вам сейчас выходить.

Садитесь, пожалуйста.

Спасибо, я постою.

Сколько стоит билет?

Я потерял билет.

До театра ещё три остановки.

Hotels

Democratization in the former Soviet Union has attracted many foreigners. Cities which were once "closed" under the communist regime are now accessible to foreign tourists and businessmen. Several hotels in major cities have been renovated to accommodate foreign guests.

Some of the hotels accept only foreign currency. The service personnel in these hotels usually speak English.

Check In

Excuse me. I have reservations.	Izvinitye. U minyá zabraníravan nómir.
I need a single room, a twin room.	Mnyé núzhin nómir na adnavo, na dvaíkh.
How much is a room per day?	Skól'ka stóit nómir vdyén?
Is there a bathroom in the room?	Vnómirye yest' tualyét?
I need three rooms on the first floor.	Mnyé núzhna tri nómira na pyérvam etazhé.
I don't want a room facing the street.	Yá ni khachú nómir, katóry vykhódit na úlitsu.
I'll stay here for three days.	Yá pravidú zdyes' tri dnya.

Check Out

Please connect me with the main desk.	Sayidinítye minyá, pazhálusta sadministrátsiyey
Could you please make out my bill?	Vy ni maglí by prigatóvit' moy shchyót?
May I leave my luggage here?	Mózhna astávit' zdyes' moy bagázh?

More about hotel accommodations

T
I
P
S

Even in major cities, there are not very many hotels, and the ones that exist are usually full. Foreign business people and Russians visiting on business from other cities are the ones who stay in hotels. In major cities, there are several hotels that offer services and accommodations similar to those of the most prestigious hotels in the West. These hotels' prices are also comparable.

Key Words

	hotel	gastínitsa	гостиница
Извините. У меня забронирован номер.	service	abslúzhivaniye	обслуживание
Мне нужен номер на одного, на двоих.	reserve a room	zabraníravat' nómir	забронировать номер
	room rate	tsiná nómira	цена номера
Сколько стоит номер в день?	single room	nómir na adnavó	номер на одного
В номере есть туалет?	double room	nómir na dvaíkh	номер на двоих
Мне нужно три номера на первом этаже.	Hotel Metropol	gastínitsa Mitrapól	гостиница Метрополь
	business hours	chisý rabóty	часы работы
Я не хочу номер, который выходит на улицу.	administra-tion	administrátsiya	администрация
Я проведу здесь три дня.	leave (on foot, by vehicle)	ukhadít', uyezhát'	уходить, уезжать
	bathroom	vánhaya kómnata	ванная комната
Соедините меня, пожалуйста, с администрацией.	hot water	garyáchaya vadá	горячая вода
	cold water	khalódnaya vadá	холодная вода
Вы не могли бы приготовить мой счёт?	bill	shchyot	счёт
	room number	nómir kómnaty	номер комнаты
Можно оставить здесь мой багаж?	upstairs	navirkhú	наверху
	downstairs	vnizú	внизу

**T
I
P
S**

Electricity in Russia is 220 volts, unlike that of the United States (110 volts). If you are planning to take electrical appliances with you, make sure to buy a converter or appliances specifically designed for Europe.

You can buy American newspapers such as *The New York Times, The Wall Street Journal,* or *The Washington Post* in hotels where foreign businessmen and tourists usually stay.

I'll leave at 2:00 P.M.	Ya uyizháyu vdva chisá dnya.

Service

Please bring my luggage to the room.	Prinisítye, pazhálusta, moy bagázh vnómir.
When do you serve breakfast?	Va skól'ka záftrak?
May I order breakfast in my room?	Mózhna zakazát' záftrak fnómir?
Please give me one more blanket.	Dáytye, pazhálusta, ishchó adnó adiyála.
There is no soap in my room.	V mayóm nómirye nyet mýla.
Please wake me up at 6:00 in the morning.	Razbudítye minyá, pazhálusta, fshest' utra.
The heat is not working in my room.	Vmayóm nómirye ni rabotayet ataplyéniye.
I can't open the window in my room.	Yá ni magú atkrýt' aknó vmayéy kómnatye.
How do I make a long distance phone call?	Kak mnye pazvanít' vdrugóy górat?

Resorts

T
H
P
S

When Russians go to resort areas on vacation they rent a room or stay at camping sites or in resorts (which include three meals a day and entertainment). People with health problems such as heart disease or ulcers can purchase a vacation package at special resorts with medical supervision and the therapy needed to treat their problems. These resorts are called *sanatoriy* (not to be confused with sanatoriums in the U.S.).

Я уезжаю в два часа дня.

Принесите, пожалуйста, мой багаж в номер.

Во сколько завтрак?

Можно заказать завтрак в номер?

Дайте, пожалуйста, ещё одно одеяло.

В моём номере нет мыла.

Разбудите меня, пожалуйста, в шесть утра.

В моём номере не работает отопление.

Я не могу открыть окно в моей комнате.

Как мне позвонить в другой город?

Key Words

floor (e.g., 1st floor)	itázh	этаж
TV	tilivízar	телевизор
refrigerator	khaladíl'nik	холодильник
breakfast	záftrak	завтрак
lunch	abyéd	обед
supper	úzhin	ужин
ice water	vadá sal'dóm	вода со льдом
towel	palatyéntse	полотенце
clean	chísty	чистый
dirty	gryázny	грязный
break	slamátsa	сломаться
take a bath	prinimát' vánnu	принимать ванну
soap	mýla	мыло
key	klyúch	ключ
blanket	adiyála	одеяло
dry cleaning	khimchístka	химчистка
stamp	márka	марка
envelope	kanvyért	конверт
airmail	ávia póchta	авиа почта
postcard	atkrýtka	открытка
parcel	pasýlka	посылка
address	ádryes	адрес
first name	ímya	имя
last name	familiya	фамилия

Vacation spots

T I P S Russians receive a total of 24 vacation days. A stay at a resort is for either 12 or 24 days. The favorite vacation time is in summer, and the most popular vacation spots are on the Black Sea. During the last few years, the prices of train and plane tickets, rent, and vacation packages have gone up significantly. People who cannot afford to spend their vacations on the Black Sea choose vacation spots along the local rivers, lakes, or camping sites.

How much does it cost per minute?

Skól'ka stóit minúta?

How do I make a call to the U.S.A.?

Kak mnye pazvanít' fse shye á?

I would like to send a telegram.

Ya khatyél (m.)/khatyéla by (f.) paslát' tiligrámmu.

Could I do it over the phone?

Mózhna zdyélat' éta pa tilifónu?

Could you help me please?

Vy mnye ni pamózhitye?

Barbershops

I need a haircut.

Mnye núzhna pastríchsya.

I like it short.

Mnyé nrávitsa karótkaya strízhka.

Not too short, please.

Pazhálusta, ni óchin' kóratka.

Please just trim it.

Tól'ka padravnyáyte, pazhálusta.

How much does a permanent cost?

Skól'ka stóit pyermanyént?

Could you blow–dry it please?

Vy ni maglí by pasushít' vólasy fyénam?

The hair dryer is too hot.

Fyen óchin' garyáchiy.

I'd like my hair dyed a darker color.

Ya khatyél (m.)/khatyéla (f.) by pakrásit' vólasy vbóliye tyómny tsvyét.

I like this hair style.

Mnye nrávitsa éta prichyóska.

What You May Hear

Kagdá vy priyékhali (prilityéli)?

When did you arrive?

Сколько стоит
минута?

Как мне позвонить
в С.Ш.А.?

Я хотел/хотела
бы послать
телеграмму.

Можно сделать это
по телефону?

Вы мне не
поможете?

Мне нужно
постричься.

Мне нравится
короткая стрижка.

Пожалуйста, не
очень коротко.

Только
подровняйте,
пожалуйста.

Сколько стоит
перманент?

Вы не могли бы
посушить волосы
феном?

Фен очень горячий.

Я хотел, хотела бы
покрасить волосы в
более тёмный цвет.

Мне нравится эта
причёска.

Когда вы приехали
(прилетели)?

Key Words

exchange	abmyén	обмен
operator	apirátar	оператор
line is busy	zányita	занята
wait	zhdat'	ждать
long distance	myezhduga-ródny	междугород-ный
there is no answer	niktó ni atvicháyet	никто не отвечает
the phone doesn't work	tilifón ni rabótayet	телефон не работает
telephone	tilifón	телефон
number	nómir	номер
haircut	strízhka	стрижка
wash hair	myt' gólavu	мыть голову
dye hair	krásit' vólasy	красить волосы

Váshe ímya i famíliya, pazhálusta.	Your first and last name please.
Kak vas zavút?	What's your name?
Padazhdítye, pazhálusta.	Please wait a second.
Zányita.	The line is busy.
Minútku.	Hold on.
Niktó ni atvicháyet.	There is no answer.
U vas zabraníravana kómnata?	Do you have a reservation?
Vash ádres fse shye á?	Your address in the U.S.A.?
Skól'ka dnyey vy sabiráyityes' zdyés' zhit'?	How many days will you be staying here?
Kagdá vy uyizháitye?	When are you leaving?
Vot vash klyuch.	Here is your key.

Ваше имя и фамилия,
пожалуйста.

Как вас зовут?

Подождите, пожалуйста.

Занято.

Минутку.

Никто не отвечает.

У вас забранирована комната.

Ваш адрес в США?

Сколько дней вы собираетесь
здесь жить?

Когда вы уезжаете?

Вот ваш ключ.

Food

вкусно!

Every major hotel in Russia has a restaurant downstairs. The main meal in Russia is dinner, which is usually eaten between 1:00 P.M. and 3:00 P.M. Usually dinner consists of a soup, main course and dessert with coffee, tea or compote (a cold, sweet drink with dry fruit). Russians drink mineral water with their meals.

During the last few years, many new private restaurants have opened in every major city. The food in these restaurants is much better but more expensive than in state-owned restaurants.

59

Breakfast in a Restaurant

Would you please bring a menu? — Prinisítye, pazhálusta minýu.

Hard boiled eggs, oatmeal and coffee, please. — Krutyýe yátsa, gyerkulyésavuyu káshu i kófe, pazhálusta.

We don't have oatmeal. — U nas nyet gerkulyésavoy káshy.

Then cream of wheat, please. — Tagdá, pazhálusta, mánnuyu káshu.

Making Reservations

Do you take reservations? — U vas mózhna zakazát' stólik?

For how many people? — Na skól'ka chilavyék?

I need a table for four, at 7:00 P.M., please. — Mnye núzhin stólik na chitvirýkh na syem' vyéchira.

Dinner at the Restaurant

Could we have a menu, please? — Minýu, pazhálusta.

What do you recommend? — Shto vy parikamindúyite?

ℾ The water

Russians do not usually drink or serve water with meals. Instead, they drink mineral water or even fruit juice. Distilled water and spring water are unavailable. Tap water is generally boiled, then cooled, and kept in glass pitchers for drinking.

Key Words

Принесите, пожалуйста, меню.	breakfast	záftrak	завтрак
	dinner	abyét	обед
Крутые яйца, геркулесовую кашу и кофе, пожалуйста.	supper	úzhin	ужин
	waiter	afitsiánt	официант
	waitress	afitsiántka	афициантка
У нас нет геркулесовой каши.	menu	minyú	меню
	like	nrávi'tsa	нравиться
Тогда, пожалуйста, манную кашу.	don't like	ní nrávitsa	не нравиться
	table	stol	стол
	napkin	salfyétka	салфетка
У вас можно заказать столик?	restaurant	ristarán	ресторан
	café	kafé	кафе
На сколько человек?	cafeteria	kafityériy	кафетерий
	bread	khlyép	хлеб
	egg	yiytsó	яйцо
Мне нужен столик на четверых на семь вечера.	fried eggs	yaíchnitsa-glazún'ya	яичница–глазунья
	hard-boiled eggs	krutýye yáytsa	крутые яйца
	soft-boiled eggs	yáytsa fsmyátku	яйца всмятку
Меню, пожалуйста.	ham	vitchiná	ветчина
Что вы порекомендуете?	butter	másla	масло

When invited to dinner . . .

If you are invited for a typical Russian dinner, you won't see hors d'oeuvres or cocktails served before dinner. Most of the time, people have a sit-down dinner starting with appetizers such as the famous Stalichniy salad (similar to German potato salad), herring, green salad (in summer and fall), or *vinegret*—a salad of cooked carrots, beets, potatoes, and dill pickles. After the main course comes dessert, which, in restaurants, is usually coffee and ice cream. Russians drink vodka and wine with their meals. Cocktails are rare.

Russians dress up for almost all social occasions. Men usually wear a tie and suit, and women wear a nice blouse, sweater, dress, or slacks.

What is your specialty?	Kakóye u vas fírminnoye blyúda?
For an appetizer, I'll take *stolichny* salad, then borscht.	Na zakúsku ya vaz'mú stalíchny salát, a patóm borshch.
Is this dish very spicy?	Eta blýuda ochin' óstraye?
I'll take stuffed cabbage (golubtsy) or beef Stroganoff as the main course.	Ya vaz'mú galubtsý ili bifstróganaf na ftaróye.
Coffee and ice cream for dessert.	Kófye i marózhenoye na disyért.
May I have ice water, please?	Mózhna vadý sal'dóm pazhálsta.
Could you bring more bread, please?	Prinisítye, pazhálsta, yishchó khlyéba.
What kind of mineral water do you have?	Kakáya minirál'naya vadá u vas yést'?
A bottle of red wine, please.	Butýlku krásnava viná, pazhálusta.

Restaurants

In Russia, don't miss the chance to try Siberian pelmeni—meat dumplings with butter or sour cream sauce.

In restaurants, the tip is usually 10% or 15%. However, Russian waiters and waitresses do not come over to the customers after the meal is served to ask if they are satisfied. Also, waiters and waitresses come by only once to take your order, so you have to order everything the first time.

In big cities, you can find restaurants that specialize in the cuisine of all the former Soviet republics.

Какое у вас
фирменное блюдо?

На закуску я
возьму столичный
салат, а потом
борщ.

Это блюдо очень
острое?

Я возьму голубцы
или беф-строганов
на второе.

Кофе и мороженое
на десерт.

Можно воды со
льдом,
пожалуйста?

Принесите,
пожалуйста, еще
хлеба.

Какая
минеральная вода
у вас есть?

Бутылку красного
вина, пожалуйста.

Key Words

milk	malakó	молоко
fish	rýba	рыба
meat	myása	мясо
chicken	kúritsa	курица
beef	gavyádina	говядина
soup	sup	суп
sandwich	butirbrót	бутерброд
tea	chay	чай
coffee	kófye	кофе
water	vadá	вода
fork	vílka	вилка
knife	nosh	нож
spoon	lóshka	ложка
orange juice	apil'sínavy sok	апельсиновый сок
mineral water	minirál'naya vadá	минеральная вода
ice cream	marózhinaye	мороженое
to your health	za váshe zdaróv'ye	за ваше здоровье
drink	pit'	пить
eat	yest'	есть
hot	garyáchiy	горячий
cold	khalódny	холодный

What produce is available?

Fruits and vegetables are usually sold only in season. They are sold in specialized state-owned "Fruit and Vegetable" stores, privately-owned stores, and the farmers' markets. The prices at the private stores and farmers' markets are much higher than in the state stores. Sometimes you can buy fresh fruits out of season in private stores or markets.

Restaurants in Russia close at 11:00 P.M. or 12:00 A.M. However, few hotels have bars that stay open all night. Many Russian restaurants have an orchestra and a dance floor. People dance and listen to music while they are having dinner.

The check, please.	Shchyót, pazhálusta.

Looking for a Restaurant

I am starving.	Ya óchin' khachú yest'.
Is there a restaurant nearby?	Yést' li gdyé-nibút' ristarán nidalikó atsyúda?
Not too expensive.	Ni óchen' daragóy.
How do you get there?	Kák tudá dayékhat'?
Is it far from here?	On dalikó atsydúda?
Do you have to go there by car?	Tudá núzhna yékhat' na mashínye?
How long will it take to go there by foot?	Skól'va vryémini tudá ittí pishkóm?
What's the name of the restaurant?	Kak nazyvayítsa ristarań?
Is there a place where we can have a quick meal?	Zdyes' mózhna gdyénibút' býstra payest'?
You can have a quick meal in a dumpling shop, a shish-kebab shop, a pancake house, a *cheburechnaya* or a Snack bar.	Býstra payést' mózhna: fpil'myénay, fshashlichnay, vblínay, fchiburyéchnay, ili vzakúsachnay.

What You May Hear

Skól'ka chilavyék?	How many people?
Sadítyes, pazhálusta.	Please sit down.
Minyú, pazhálusta.	Menu, please.
Stalíchniy salát	Stolichny salad (similar to German potato salad)
Salát iz pamidór	Tomato salad
Avashchnóy salát	Vegetable salad

Счёт, пожалуйста.

Я очень хочу есть.

Есть ли где–нибудь
ресторан недалеко
отсюда?

Не очень дорогой.

Как туда доехать?

Он далеко отсюда?

Туда нужно ехать
на машине?

Сколько времени
туда идти пешком?

Как называется
ресторан?

Здесь можно где–
нибудь быстро
поесть?

Быстро поесть
можно в
Пельменной, в
Шашлычной, в
Блинной, в
Чебуречной или в
Закусочной.

Сколько человек?

Садитесь,
пожалуйста.

Меню, пожалуйста.

Столичный салат

Салат из помидор

Овощной салат

Key Words

spicy	óstry	острый
salty	salyóny	солёный
salt	sol'	соль
sweet	slátkiy	сладкий
sugar	sákhar	сахар
fruits	frúkty	фрукты
apple	yáblaka	яблоко
orange	apil'sín	апельсин
pear	grúsha	груша
banana	banán	банан
watermelon	arbús	арбуз
melon	dýnya	дыня
vegetables	óvashchi	овощи
tomato	pamidór	помидор
cucumber	aguryéts	огурец
carrot	markóf'	морковь
potatoes	kartófel'	картофель
onions	luk	лук
radishes	ridíska	редиска
caviar	ikrá	икра
black caviar	chyórnaya	чёрная икра
red caviar	krásnaya ikrá	красная икра
salad	salát	салат
dessert	disyért	десерт
for dessert	na disyért	на десерт

Borshch	Beet soup
Shchi	Cabbage soup
Avashchnóy sup	Vegetable soup
Sup slapshóy i skúritsey.	Chicken noodle soup
Rýba skartófil'nym pyuré	Fish with mashed potatoes
Katlyéty s zhárinoy kartóshkoy	Cutlets with french fries
Bifstróganaf	Beef Stroganoff
Shashlýk	Shish-kebab
Pil'myéni	Steamed dumplings
Zhárinaya kúritsa	Fried chicken
Atbivnáya	Steak
Svínyye atbivnyye	Pork chops
Galuptsý	Stuffed cabbage
Shnítzel'	Schnitzel
Kófye	Coffee
Chay	Tea
Minirál'naya vadá	Mineral water
Kvas	Kvas (drink)
Vinó	Wine
Byélaye vinó	White wine
Krásnaye vinó	Red wine
Píva	Beer

Борщ

Щи

Овощной суп

Суп с лапшой и с курицей

Рыба с картофельным пюре

Котлéты с жаренной
картошкой

Биф–Строганов

Шашлык

Пельмени

Жаренная курица

Отбивная

Свинные отбивные

Голубцы

Шницель

Кофе

Чай

Минеральная вода

Квас

Вино

Белое вино

Красное вино

Пиво

Shopping

You will probably want to buy famous Russian souvenirs, such as *matryóshki* (nesting dolls), lacquer boxes, balalaikas, Russian fur hats, wooden Easter eggs, and amber. You can purchase these items in souvenir stores, some of which are located in the hotels.

Arbát Street in Moscow is a big souvenir bazaar. Make sure you also visit Russia's largest department store, *GUM*, located on Red Square, and the art and souvenir bazaar in *Izmáilovo*.

The *Izmáilovo* bazaar is open only on Saturdays and Sundays. There are also special stores where only foreign currency is accepted. Remember that most Russian stores close from 1:00 P.M. to 2:00 P.M., or from 2:00 P.M. to 3:00 P.M. for lunch.

In the Department Store

Please show me that shirt.	Pakazhítye, pazhálusta, ety rubáshku.
What size is this?	Kakóy eta razmyér?
Do you have any other color?	U vas yest' drugóy tsvyét?
I'd like something bright.	Ya khachú shtó-nibut' yárkaye.
Please show me that red sweater.	Pakazhítye, pazhálusta, état krásny svítar.
Do you have a larger size?	U vas yest' ból'shiy razmyér?
I don't like this color.	Mnye ni nrávitsa etat tsvyet.
Can you show me another color?	Vy ni maglí by pakazát' mnye drugóy tsvyet?
May I try it on?	Mózhna pamyérit'?
It fits well.	On kharashoˊsidít.
I'll take it.	Ya vaz'múv yivó.
How much is it?	Skól'ka stóit?
One thousand rubles.	Týsyacha rublyéy.
I like this blouse.	Mnye nrávitsa eta blúska.

The challenge of shopping

T
I
P
S

Shopping is a big challenge for Russians. People do not buy things when they need them but rather when they see them in the store, because of chronic shortages. When the state-owned department stores haves sales on "hard-to-get items" such as women's winter boots, wool sweaters, children's clothes, and home appliances, there are always long lines that last for hours.

Key Words

Покажите, пожалуйста, эту рубашку.

Какой это размер?

У вас есть другой цвет?

Я хочу что-нибудь яркое.

Покажите, пожалуйста, этот красный свитер.

У вас есть больший размер?

Мне не нравится этот цвет.

Вы не могли бы показать мне другой цвет?

Можно померить?

Он хорошо сидит.

Я возьму его.

Сколько стоит?

Тысяча рублей.

Мне нравится эта блузка.

souvenir	suvinír	сувенир
amber	yantár'	янтарь
like (v.)	nrávitsa	нравиться
price	tsiná	цена
receipt	chyek	чек
silk	sholk	шёлк
shirt	rubáshka	рубашка
blouse	blúzka	блузка
sweater	svitr	свитер
size	razmýer	размер
ring	kal'tsó	кольцо
earrings	syér'gi	серьги
necklace	búsy, tsipóchka	бусы, цепочка
color	tsvyet	цвет
to want	khatyét'	хотеть
I want	ya khachú	я хочу
store	magazín	магазин
bookstore	knízhny magazín	книжный магазин
newspaper	gazyéta	газета
magazine	zhurnál	журнал
map	kárta	карта
tourist	turíst	турист
book	kníga	книга
foreign languages	inastrányye yazykí	иностранные языки

Private stores

During the last few years, many small private stores have begun to sell imported clothing, televisions, VCR's, and other goods for approximately the same prices as in the West, which by Russian standards are extremely expensive.

Is it silk?	Eta sholk?
What size is that?	Kakóy razmyér?
My size is 36.	Moy razmyér trídsadtz shest'.
Do you have one with long sleeves?	U vas yest' zdlínym rukavóm?
I like these silk ties.	Myne nrávitsa eti shyólkavyye gálstuki.
Do you have a different color?	U vas yest' drugóy tsvyét?
I'll buy it for my husband.	Ya kuplyú mayimú múzhu.

Shopping in a Souvenir Store

Please show me that matryoshka (nesting doll).	Pakazhítye, pazhálusta, etu matryóshku.
How many dolls are in there?	Skól'ka vnyey matryóshek?
Do you have a five-doll matryoshka?	U vas yest' pitimyésnaya matryóshka?
How much?	Skól'ka stóit?
What do you call the famous Russian lacquer boxes?	Kak nazyváyitsa znaminítyye rúskiye shkatúlki?

Opening and closing times

Т
И
Р
С

There are no shopping malls and few department stores in Russia. The oldest and most popular department store is GUM, located on Moscow's Red Square. There are also many smaller specialty stores in Moscow that sell shoes, clothing, cosmetics, and books.

Grocery stores are open from 9:00 A.M. to 8:00 or 10:00 P.M., but they close for lunch from 1:00 P.M. to 2:00 P.M. Department stores are open from 8:00 A.M. to 9:00 P.M. Small gift shops and consumer-goods stores are open from 11:00 A.M. to 8:00 P.M. and close for lunch from 2:00 P.M. to 3:00 P.M.

Это шёлк?

Какой размер?

Мой размер 36.

У вас есть с длинным рукавом?

Мне нравятся эти шёлковые галстуки.

У вас есть другой цвет?

Я куплю моему мужу.

Покажите, пожалуйста, эту матрёшку.

Сколько в ней матрёшек?

У вас есть пятиместная матрёшка?

Сколько стоит?

Как называются знаменитые русские шкатулки?

Key Words

buy (v.)	pakupát', kupit'	покупать, купить
five hundred rubles	pitsót rublyéy	пятьсот рублей
thousand rubles	týsyachia rublyéy	тысяча рублей

Handicrafts

Tourists especially like to buy handicrafts such as wood carvings, painted wooden souvenirs, and ceramics. Russian lace bedspreads, pillowcases, and napkins also make wonderful souvenirs. Bright wooden spoons, cups, goblets, and trays decorated with black paint on a golden background are works of Khokhloma craftsmen. This art has been passed down from generation to generation for more than 300 years.

Pálekhskiye shkatúlki.	Palékhskiye shkatúlki.
I would like to buy one.	Ya khatýel (m.)/khatyéla (f.) by kupít' adnú.
Where are they made?	Gdye ikh dyélayut?
Would you please give me a receipt.	Dáytye mnye, pazhálusta, chyek.
Can they be taken out of the country with a receipt?	Ikh mózhna vyvazít' iz straný s chékom?
I also would like to buy amber.	Ya tákzhe khatél (m.)/khatyéla (f.) by kupít' yantár'.
I have heard that most amber comes from the Baltic countries.	Ya znáyu, shto vasnavnóm yantár' privózyat iz Baltískikh stran.
Is it true that the city of Kaliningrad is considered the amber capital?	Eta pravda, shto górat Kaliningrad shchitáyitsa stalítsy yantaryá?
I would like to buy a matching set: a ring, earrings and a necklace.	Mne khóchetsa kupít' garnitúr: kal'tsó, syér'gi i búsy.

Buying Books and Newspapers

Where can I buy English books and newspapers?	Gdye mózhna kupít' knígi i gazyéty na anglískam yizikyé?
Where is the foreign language bookstore?	Gdye magazín knik na inastránnykh yizikákh?
I think the store in Moscow is called *Friendship*.	Ya dúmayu, shto magazín vMaskvyé nazyváitsa *Drúzhba*.
Do you have any American magazines?	U vas yest' amyerikánskiye zhurnály?
Do you have a Russian newspaper in English?	U vas yest' rússkaya gazyéta na anglískam yizykyé?
Do you have any books for tourists?	U vas yest' knígi dlya turístaf?
I need a map of Moscow.	Mne nuzhná kárta Maskvý.
Do you have children's books?	U vas yest' dyétskiye knigi?

Палехские шкатулки.

Я хотел/хотела бы купить одну.

Где их делают?

Дайте мне, пожалуйста, чек.

Их можно вывозить из страны с чеком?

Я также хотел/хотела бы купить янтарь.

Я знаю, что в основном янтарь привозят из Балтийских стран.

Это правда, что город Калининград считается столицей янтаря?

Мне хочется купить гарнитур: кольцо, серьги и бусы.

Где можно купить книги и газеты на русском языке?

Где магазин книг на иностранных языках?

Я думаю что магазин в Москве называется „Дружба.“

У вас есть американские журналы?

У вас есть русская газета на английском языке?

У вас есть книги для туристов?

Мне нужна карта Москвы.

У вас есть детские книги?

I want to buy books for my kids.	Ya khatyél (m.)/khatyéla (f.) by kupít' knígi maím dyétyam.

At the Farmer's Market

How much are the red apples? One kilo, please.	Skól'ka stóyat krásnyye yáblaki? Kilagrámm, pazhálusta.
The grapes look very fresh. Do they come from Georgia?	Vinagrát takóy svyézhiy. Yevó privizlí iz Grúzii?
Would you put the grapes in the bag?	Vy ni maglí by palazhít' vinagrát fpakyét?
I want to buy a melon. It is delicious.	Ya khachú kupít' dýnyu. Oná óchin' fkúsnaya.

What You May Hear

Kharashó sidít.	It fits you well.
Kakóy razmyér?	What size?
Kakóy tsvyet?	What color?
Vsyo raspródano.	All sold out.
Kakóy (m.)/kakáya (f.)/kakóye (n.)?	Which one?
Vam idyót état tsvyet.	This color becomes you.
Vot vash chyek.	Here is your receipt.
U nas nyet yantaryá sichás.	We don't have amber now.

Я хотел, хотела бы купить
книги моим детям.

Сколько стоят красные
яблоки? Килограмм,
пожалуйста.

Виноград такой свежий. Его
привезли из Грузии?

Вы не могли бы положить
виноград в пакет?

Я хочу купить дыню. Она
очень вкусная.

Хорошо сидит.

Какой размер?

Какой цвет?

Всё распродано.

Какой/какая/какое?

Вам идёт этот цвет.

Вот ваш чек.

У нас нет янтаря сейчас.

Making Friends

Russian may appear unfriendly to visitors.

They don't smile to strangers and it is hard to catch their eye. But in reality, Russians are a very friendly and hospitable people. They try to understand you and will go out of their way to help with directions, or to answer your questions.

Meeting for the First Time

Hello.	Zdrástvuytye.
I am an American.	Ya amyerikányets (m.).
Have you been to the States before?	Vy býli v Shtátakh rán'she?
I like Moscow.	Mnye nrávitsa Maskvá.
I want to speak Russian.	Ya khochú gavarít' pa rúski.
Can you tutor me?	Vy ni maglí by samnóy zanimátsa?
I speak very little Russian.	Ya nimnóga gavaryú pa rúski.
I don't understand.	Ya ni panimáyu.
Please say it again.	Paftarítye, pazhálusta.
How old are you?	Skól'ka vam lyet?
Are you married?	Vy zhináty? (m.)/Vy zámuzhim? (f.)
Do you have any children?	U vas yest' dyéti?
Where do you work?	Gdye vy rabótaitye?

Some etiquette

T If you are invited to visit someone's home, bring a small gift—a box
I of chocolate or flowers, for example, or a souvenir from the U.S.
P   If you happen to be at someone's home at lunch or dinnertime,
S people will invite you to join them. Even if you refuse politely, the
   invitation will probably be repeated several times. Russians can be
   very persistent when they are making an invitation or offering
   somebody something.

Key Words

Russian	English	pronunciation	Russian
Здравствуйте.	weather	pagóda	погода
Я американец.	cold	khóladna	холодно
Вы были в Штатах раньше?	hot	zhárka	жарко
	warm	tipló	тепло
	rainy	dazhdlívy	дождливый
Мне нравится Москва.	windy	vyétriny	ветренный
	work (v)	rabótat'	работать
Я хочу говорить по-русски.	work (n)	rabóta	работа
	to be married	byt' zámuzhim (f.)	быть замужем
Вы не могли бы со мной заниматься?		byt' zhinátym (m.)	быть женатым
Я немного говорю по-русски.	children	dyéti	дети
	engineer	inzhinyér	инженер
Я не понимаю.	medical doctor	vrách, dóktar	врач, доктор
Повторите, пожалуйста.	lawyer	yuríst	юрист
	teacher	uchítyel' (m.)	учитель
Сколько вам лет?		uchítyel'nitsa (f.)	учительница
Вы женаты?/Вы замужем?	invite	priglasít'	пригласить
	free time	svabódnaye vryémya	свободное время
У вас есть дети?	smoke	kurít'	курить
Где вы работаете?			

The Bolshoi Theater

Т
П
Р
S

The Bolshoi Theater attracts large numbers of tourists in Russia. Originally built in 1824, the Bolshoi is famous for its ballet and opera performances. Among these performances are ballets and operas from the 19th century by the founders of Russian classical music—Glinka, Tchaikovsky, and Borodin—as well as contemporary performances. The Bolshoi Theater is still totally subsidized by the state.

Evening performances at all theaters begin at 7:00 P.M. or 7:30 P.M. Theater-goers usually check their coats at the theater free of charge.

Introductory Remarks

May I please introduce Mr. Ivanov?	Razrishítye pridstávit' gaspadína Ivanóva.
It is very nice to meet you.	Óchin' priyátna paznakómitsa.
I'm John Smith.	Ya Dzhon Smit.
When did you arrive?	Kagdá vy priyékhali?
I arrived yesterday morning.	Ya priyékhal fchyerá útram.
Where are you staying?	Gdye vy astanavílis'?
At the Intourist hotel.	Vgastínitsye Inturíst.
This is my first time in Russia.	Ya pyérvy ras vRassíi.
Goodbye.	Da svidániya.
See you later.	Uvídimsya.

Invitations

I have tickets to the ballet for tomorrow. Would you like to go with me?	U minyá yest' bilyéty na balyét na záftra. Vy ni khatyéli by payti samnóy?

Recreation

Russian families usually spend the little free time they have visiting friends and relatives, shopping, watching TV, going to the movies, and reading. Because of shortages and high prices for food, clothing, and lack of kitchen appliances, shopping and housework take a lot of time away from recreation activities.

Nevertheless, in winter, people find time for skiing, and youngsters everywhere can be seen skating, while in summer, boys and young men spend a lot of time playing soccer. Soccer and hockey are exclusively male sports in Russia, while badminton is a popular family sport.

Key Words

Разрешите
представить
господина Петрова.

Очень приятно
познакомиться.

Я Джон Смит.

Когда вы приехали?

Я приехал вчера
утром.

Где вы
остановились?

В гостинице
Интурист.

Я первый раз в
России.

До свидания.

Увидимся.

У меня есть билеты
на балет на завтра.
Вы не хотели бы
пойти со мной?

hotel	gastínitsa	гостиница
trip	payéztka, putishéstviye	поездка, путешествие
gift	padárak	подарок
telephone	tilifón	телефон
number	nómir	номер
address	ádryes	адрес
I'll call later	pazvanyú, pózhe	позвоню позже
just a moment	adnú minútachku	одну минуточку
please wait	padazhdítye, pazhálusta	подождите, пожалуйста
music	múzyka	музыка
dance	tantsivát'	танцевать
painting	kartíńa	картина
sport	sport	спорт
play chess	igrat' fshákhmaty	играть в шахматы
movie	kinó, fil'm	кино, фильм
fish	lavít' rýbu	ловить рыбу
travel	putishéstvavat'	путешествовать
friend	druk	друг

I'm afraid I can't.

Bayús' shto nyet.

I am going to a birthday party.

Ya idú na dyen' razhdyéniya.

Do you want tea or coffee?

Vy khatítye chay ili kófye?

What do you want to drink?
Beer, juice, mineral water, wine, vodka?

Shto vy khatítye pit'? Píva, sok, minerál'nuyu vódu, vinó, vótku?

Would you like to see a movie?

Khatítye paytí fkinó?

Yes. I would love to.

Da óchin' khachú.

You are invited to a reception on Monday.

Vy priglashíný na priyóm fpanidyél'nik.

Calling on Someone

May I come in?

Mózhna vaytí?

Please come in.

Zakhadítye, pazhálusta.

Sorry I'm late.

Izvinítye za apazdániye.

I haven't seen you for ages.

Ni vídyel vas sto lyet.

It's cold/hot today.

Sivódnya khóladna/zhárka.

I am very pleased to see you.

Ya óchin' rad vas vidit'.

You haven't changed. You look just the same.

Vy ni izminílis'. Výgliditye tákzhe.

Do you mind if I smoke?

Vy ni vazrazháyitye, yésli ya zakuryú?

Of course not.

Kanyéshna, nyet.

Are you busy?

Vy zányaty?

I would like to invite you to my house.

Ya khachú priglasít' vas ksibyé damóy.

Are you free of Tuesday?

Vy svabódny vaftórnik?

Unfortunately, I don't have time on Tuesday.

Ksazhilyéniyu, u minyá nyet vryémini vaftórnik.

And on Wednesday?

A fsryédu?

I have a small present for you.

U minyá est' dlya vas nibal'shóy padárak.

Боюсь, что нет.

Я иду на день рождения.

Вы хотите чай или кофе?

Что вы хотите пить? Пиво,
сок, минеральную воду, вино,
водку?

Хотите пойти в кино?

Да очень хочу.

Вы приглашены на приём в
понедельник.

Можно войти?

Заходите, пожалуйста.

Извините за опоздание.

Не видел вас сто лет.

Сегодня холодно/жарко.

Я очень рад вас видеть.

Вы не изменились. Выглядете
так же.

Вы не возражаете, если я
закурю?

Конечно, нет.

Вы заняты?

Я хочу пригласить вас к себе
домой.

Вы свободны во вторник?

К сожалению, у меня нет
времени во вторник.

А в среду?

У меня есть для вас небольшой
подарок.

When are you leaving?	Kagdá vy uyizzháitye?
On Thursday.	Fchitvyérk.
Have a nice trip.	Shchistlívava putí.
Please let me know when you come to the States.	Saabshchítye mnye, pazhálsta, kagdá vy priyéditye v Shtáty.
I'll pick you up at the airport.	Ya vas vstryéchu v aerapartú.

Calling a Friend on the Phone

Hello.	Alyó.
May I please speak to Sasha?	Mózhna paprasít' Sáshu ktilifónu?
Hi. This is John Smith.	Zdrástvuytye. Eta Dzhon Smit.
I've just arrived.	Ya tól'ka shto priyékhal.
How are you?	Kak pazhiváyitye?
How is your wife?	Kak vásha zhiná?
Thank you, she is fine.	Spasíba, kharashó.
I want to see you.	Ya khachú vas uvídit'.
What is your address?	Kakóy u vas ádryes?
Which bus should I take?	Na kakóy aftóbus mnye núzhna syest'?
At what stop should I get off?	Na kakóy astanófkye mnye vykhodít'?
I'll call back later.	Ya pazvanyú yishchó ras pózhe.
Please tell him/her to call me.	Piridáytye pazhálusta, shtóby on (m.)/oná (f.) mnye pazvanil (m.)/ pazvaníla (f.).
I am staying at the Intourist hotel.	Ya zhivú v gastínitsye Inturíst.
My phone number is . . .	Moy tilifón . . .

Когда вы уезжаете?

В четверг.

Счастливого пути.

Сообщите мне, пожалуйста, когда вы приедете в Штаты.

Я вас встречу в аэропорту.

Алло.

Можно попросить Сашу к телефону?

Здравствуйте. Это Джон Смит.

Я только что приехал.

Как поживаете?

Как ваша жена?

Спасибо, хорошо.

Я хочу вас увидеть.

Какой у вас адрес?

На какой автобус мне нужно сесть?

На какой остоновке мне выходить?

Я позвоню ещё раз позже.

Передайте пожалуйста, чтобы он/она мне позвонил/позвонила.

Я живу в гостинице Интурист.

Мой телефон. . .

Talking About Hobbies

What do you do in your spare time?

Shto vy dyélayetye vsvabódnaye vryémya?

I like music.
Ya lyublyú múzyku.

I like to dance.
Ya lyublyú tantsivát'.

I also like to read.
Ya tózhe lyublyú chitát'.

Sometimes I go fishing.
Inagdá ya khazhú na rybálku.

Do you like soccer?
Vam nrávitsa futból?

How do you spend your weekends?

Kak vy pravóditye vykhadnýye?

What You May Hear

Kagdá vý priyékhali?
When did you arrive?

Rad svámi paznakómitsa.
Glad to meet you.

Dabró pazhálavat'.
Welcome.

Piridáytye privyét . . .
Say hello to . . .

Vy kúritye?
Do you smoke?

Prakhadítye, pazhálusta.
Please come in.

Sadítis', pazhálusta.
Please sit down.

Papróbuytye eta, pazhálusta.
Please try this.

Gdye vy astanavílis'?
Where are you staying?

Kagdá vy uyezháyitye?
When are you leaving?

Что вы делаете в свободное время?

Я люблю музыку.
Я люблю танцевать.
Я также люблю читать.

Иногда я хожу на рыбалку.

Вам нравится футбол?

Как вы проводите выходные?

Когда вы приехали?

Рад с вами познакомиться.

Добро пожаловать.

Передайте привет . . .

Вы курите?

Проходите, пожалуйста.

Садитесь, пожалуйста.

Попробуйте это, пожалуйста.

Где вы остановились?

Когда вы уезжаете?

Entertainment

Russia offers a wide variety of entertainment for the traveler. There are concerts, folk dance performances, circuses, theaters, ballets, operas, symphonies, musicals, etc. The Bolshoi and Kirov ballets are well-known in Russia and abroad. Theatrical productions, the ballet, and the opera are especially popular with Russians. Foreign tourists might have problems understanding the singing, but the music and the acting make a visit to the opera a worthwhile experience.

Watching a Performance

When do we go to the Bolshoi Theater?	Kagdá my idyóm vBal'shóy tiátr?
What's on tonight?	Shto sivódnya idyót?
What is it called?	Kak nazyváyitsa?
I love opera.	Ya lyublyú ópiru.
Can you tell me please what this opera is about?	Vy ni maglí by raskazát' mnye a chým éta ópira?
Is there a synopsis of the story in English?	Yest' li apisániye dyéystviya ópiri na anglískam?
Please translate this sentence.	Pirividítye, pazhálusta, éta pridlazhéniye.
Is this singer famous?	État pivyéts izvyésny?
I want to see Russian folk dances.	Ya khachú pasmatryét' rússkiye naródnyye tantsy.
What time does the concert start?	Va skól'ka nachináyetsa kantsyeŕt?
Hurry up!	Bystryéye!
The performance will start soon.	Spyektákl' skóra nachnyótsa.

More entertainment

$\mathbb{T}$
$\mathbb{\Pi}$
$\mathbb{P}$
$\mathbb{S}$

Theaters and movies are very popular in Russia. Although ticket prices have increased tremendously, Russians still find time and money for a good show. There are many European, Mexican, and American movies dubbed in Russian.

Movies are among the most popular forms of entertainment, and international film festivals, which take place once every two years in Moscow, are a big cultural event. For a whole week, you can see movies from almost every country in the world.

Key Words

Когда мы идём в
Большой театр?

Что сегодня идёт?

Как называется?

Я люблю оперу.

Вы не могли бы
рассказать мне о
чём эта опера?

Есть ли описание
действия оперы на
английском?

Переведите,
пожалуйста, это
предложение.

Этот певец
известный?

Я хочу посмотреть
русские народные
танцы.

Во сколько
начинается
концерт?

Быстрее!

Спектакль скоро
начнётся.

performance	spyektákl'	спектакль
play	pyésa	пьеса
opera	ópira	опера
ballet	balýet	балет
dance (n.)	tántsy	танцы
dance (v.)	tantsivát'	танцевать
symphony	simfanícheskiy arkyéstr	симфонический оркестр
orchestra	arkyéstr	оркестр
begin, start	nachinát'	начинать
end (n.)	kanyéts	конец
end (v.)	zakánchivat'	заканчивать
actor	aktyór	актёр
actress	aktrísa	актриса
famous	znaminíty	знаменитый
introduction	fstuplyéniye	вступление
buy a ticket	pakupát' bilyét	покупать билет
return a ticket	vazvratít' bilyét	возвратить билет
intermission	antrákt	антракт
which row	kakóy ryad	какой ряд
seat	myésta	место
number	nómir	номер
orchestra seat	myésta fpartyérye	место в партере

Do you have a program of the show?	U vas yest' pragrámka spyektáklya?

Being Seated

I have an orchestra seat, fifth row.	Ya sizhú fpyátam ridú partyéra.
These are good seats. Do you have a balcony seat or rear orchestra?	Eta kharóshiye myestá. Ty sidísh na balkónye ili vamfityátrye?
Is this seat taken?	Eta myésta zányita?
You must be in the wrong seat.	Vy navyérna, sidítye ni na svayóm myéstye.
Let me pass please.	Razrishítye, pazhálusta, praytí.
Where are your seats?	Gdye váshi myestá?

After the Show

I liked the concert very much, especially the Russian folk dances.	Mnye óchin' panrávilsya kantsyért, asóbyenna russkiye naródnyye tántsy.
This is the first time I've seen the Bolshoi ballet.	Ya pérvy raz vídyel (m.)/vídyela (f.) balyét Bol'shóva tiátra.
I've never listened to Russian folk music.	Ya nikagdá ni slýshal (m.)/ slýshala (f.) rússkuyu naródnuyu múzyku.

T Folk dance performances

P Going to see Russian folk dances might well be among your most memorable experiences in Russia. Colorful costumes and melodic folk music are combined in spectacular traditional dances that date S back hundreds of years.

У вас есть
программка
спектакля?

Я сижу в пятом
ряду партера.

Это хорошие места.
Ты сидишь на
балконе или в
амфитеатре?

Это место занято?

Вы, наверное, сидите
не на своём месте.

Разрешите,
пожалуйста, пройти.

Где ваши места?

Мне очень
понравился концерт,
особенно русские
народные танцы.

Я первый раз видел/
видела балет
Большого театра.

Я никогда не
слышал/ слышала
русскую народную
музыку.

Key Words

balcony seat	myésta na balkónye	место на балконе
rear orchestra	amfityátr	амфитеатр
mezzanine	byel'etásh	бельэтаж
box	lózha	ложа
sports	spórt	спорт
game	igrá	игра
volleyball	valeyból	волейбол
football	amyerikánskiy futból	американский футбол
soccer	futból	футбол
basketball	basketból	баскетбол
tennis	tyénnis	теннис
score	shchyot	счёт

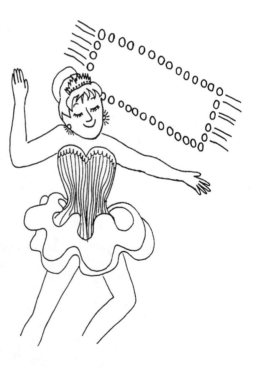

Where can I buy tapes of Russian folk music?	Gdye mózhna kupít' kasyéty srússkay naródnay múzykay?
Is Evgeni Onegin a popular opera in Russia?	Pól'zuyitsa li ópira Yevgyéniy Anyégin papulyárnast'yu v Rassii?
I don't understand a word, but the music is so beautiful that I don't need a translation.	Ya ni panimáyu ni slóva, no múzyka takáya krasívaya, shto mnye ni núzhin pirivót.

Sport Event

What sport do you like to play?	Kakím spórtam vy lyúbitye zanimátsa?
I like soccer.	Ya lyublyú futból.
I want to see a soccer match.	Ya khachú pasmatrýet' futból'ny mach.
Where can I buy a ticket?	Gdye mózhna kupít' bilyét?
How much is a ticket?	Skól'ka stóit bilyét?
May I return the ticket?	Mózhna vazvratít' bilyét?
Which teams are playing?	Kakíye kamándy igráyut?
Which team is wearing the white shirts?	Kakáya kamánda vbyélykh máykakh?
What is the score?	Kakóy shchyot?
Who is winning?	Kto vyígrivayit?

What You May Hear

Kakóy ryát?	Which row?
Kakóye myésta?	Which seat?
Idíte zamnóy, pazhálusta.	Please follow me.
Pragráma.	Program.
Vam nrávitsa?	Do you like it?
Skaryéye, my apázdyvayem.	Hurry up, we are late.

Где можно купить кассету с
русской народной музыкой?

Пользуется ли опера Евгений
Онегин популярностью в
России?

Я не понимаю ни слова, но
музыка такая красивая, что
мне не нужен перевод.

Каким спортом вы любите
заниматься?

Я люблю футбол.

Я хочу посмотреть
футбольный матч.

Где можно купить билет?

Сколько стоит билет?

Можно возвратить билет?

Какие команды играют?

Какая команда в белых
майках?

Какой счёт?

Кто выигрывает?

Какой ряд?

Какое место?

Идите за мной, пожалуйста.

Програма.

Вам нравится?

Скорее, мы опаздываем.

Sightseeing

All major cities in Russia offer a wide range of sights to see. The Kremlin, "The Heart of Russia," is one of the most impressive museums in the country. Inside the Kremlin walls you may visit cathedrals which were built in the fifteenth and sixteenth centuries, the Hall of Facets that was used for special banquets, and the Armory, Moscow's oldest museum. Other landmarks are the Tretyakov Picture Gallery, the Pushkin Museum, and the Bolshoi Theatre in Moscow; and the Hermitage Museum, the Russian Museum, and the Winter and Summer Palaces in St. Petersburg. The cathedrals and churches of Novgorod also attract tourists to Russia.

Preparing for a Trip

Where can I buy a map of Moscow?	Gdye mózhna kupít' kártu Maskvý?
Is it in English?	Aná na anglískam?
I need an English speaking tour guide.	Mnye núzhin gid gavarýashchiy paanglíski.
What places of interest can I see in your city?	Kakíye dastaprimichátil'nasti ya magú pasmatryét' vváshem góradye?
What are the plans for today?	Kakíye plány na sivódnya?
May I take pictures here?	Zdyes' mózhna fatagrafíravat'?
What time will we be back in the hotel?	Kagdá mi priyédim abrátna vgastínitsu?
How long does it take to get to the museum?	Skól'ka vryémini zanimáyit dayékhat' da muzyéya?

Museums and galleries

T
I
P
S

There are various museums and art galleries in every major city. The Tretyakov Gallery in Moscow was founded by Pavel M. Tretyakov in 1892 and has the most complete collection of works by Russian artists. However, the largest museum in Russia is the Hermitage in St. Petersburg. Founded in 1764, the Hermitage has a unique collection of paintings, graphic art, applied art, and sculptures, including masterpieces by Rubens, Rembrandt, Titian, Velazquez, Leonardo da Vinci, and Raphael.

There are several picturesque 18th- and 19th-century estates located on the outskirts of Moscow and St. Petersburg. In hotels where foreign tourists usually stay, there are offices open from 9:00 A.M. to 10:00 P.M. where you can make reservations to visit museums, art galleries, or for concerts.

Key Words

Где можно купить
карту Москвы?

Она на
английском?

Мне нужен гид
говорящий по—
английски.

Какие
достопримечательности
я могу посмотреть
в вашем городе?

Какие планы на
сегодня?

Здесь можно
фотографировать?

Когда мы приедем
обратно в
гостиницу?

Сколько времени
занимает доехать
до музея?

guide	gid	гид
schedule	raspisániye	расписание
sights	dastaprimi-chátil'nasti	достоприме-чательности
Kremlin	Kreml'	Кремль
The Hall of Facets	Granavítaya paláta	Грановитая палата
The Armory	Aruzhéynaya paláta	Оружейная палата
cathedral	kafidrálny sabór	кафедральный собор
church	tsérkaf'	церковь
picture gallery	kartínnaya galiryéya	картинная галерея
train	póyist	поезд
plane	samalyót	самолёт
take a picture	fatagrafíravat'	фотографировать
camera	fotaaparát	фотоаппарат
factory	zavót	завод
worker	rabóchiy	рабочий
employee	rabótnik	работник
salary	zarpláta	зарплата
income	dakhód	доход
work	rabótat'	работать
call a taxi	výzvat' taksí	вызвать такси

What is the weather like today?	Kakáya sivódnya pagóda?
Is it raining?	Idyót dózht'?
Should I take an umbrella?	Mnye núzhna vzyat' zont?
Should I take a sweater?	Mnye núzhna vzyat' svítr?
We would like to go to the picture gallery again.	My khatím yishchó ras paytí fkartínnuyu galiryéyu.
We would like to see . . .	My khatím pasmatryét' . . . .

Visiting a Tourist Site

When were these cathedrals built?	Kagdá bylí pastróyeny eti sabóry?
In what century was this church built?	V kakóm vyékye bylá pastróyina éta tsérkaf'?
Will we be able to go to the Armory?	My smózhim paytí vAruzhéynuyu palátu?
Is the museum open on Sunday?	Muzyéy atkrýt vvaskrisýen'ye?
How do I get to the Hermitage museum?	Kak dayékhat' da Ermitázha?
What time does it open?	Kagdá on atkryváyetsa?

Visiting a Factory (Questions you might ask the manager)

How many workers are there in the factory?	Skól'ka rabóchikh rabótayet na zavódye?
How much does a worker make a month?	Skól'ka rabóchiy palucháyet vmyésits?

ℙ The workday

In most offices and factories, people work eight hours a day, five days a week, with one hour for lunch. Workers in factories usually start work at 8:00 A.M., and office workers start at 9:00 or 9:30 A.M. Russians do not avoid talking about their salaries. They will openly tell you how much they make.

Какая сегодня погода?

Идёт дождь?

Мне нужно взять зонт?

Мне нужно взять свитр?

Мы хотим ещё раз пойти в картинную галерею.

Мы хотим посмотреть . . . .

Когда были построены эти соборы?

В каком веке была построена эта церковь?

Мы сможем пойти в Оружейную полату?

Музей открыт в воскресенье?

Как доехать до Эрмитажа?

Когда он открывается?

Сколько рабочих работает на заводе?

Сколько рабочий получает в месяц?

What do you produce?	Shto vy praizvóditye?
How much do you pay during sick leave?	Kak vy apláchivayetye bal'níchny list?
Do you pay during maternity leave?	Vy plátitye zarplátu va vryémya dikryétnava ótpuska?
Are female employees paid the same as male?	Zhénshchiny palucháyut takúyu zhe zarplátu kak i muzhchíny?
How many hours do you work a day?	Skól'ka chisóf vdyen' vy rabótayetye?

Taking Pictures

Can you please take a picture of me?	Vy ni maglí by minýa sfatagrafíravat'?
Everything is set.	Fsyo ustanóvlina.
Press the button and that's it.	Nazhmítye na knópku i fsýo.
Can I take a picture of you?	Mózhna ya vas sfatagrafíruyu?
Let's take a picture together.	Daváytye sfatagrafíruyimsya vmyéstye.
I would like to take a picture by the Pushkin monument.	Ya khachú sfatagrafíravatsa u pámyitnika Púshkinu.
Smile!	Ulybnítyes'!
Where can I have these pictures developed and printed?	Gdye mózhna prayivít' i napichátat' fatagráfii?
Please give me your address and I will send you pictures.	Dáytye, pazhálusta, vash ádryes i ya pashlyú vam fatagráfii.

Talking with a Russian Tourist

Are you a tourist, too?	Vy tózhe turíst?
Where are you from?	Atkúda vy?
Is Tula an interesting city for tourists?	Túla intiryésny górat dlya turístaf?
Can I get there by train?	Tudá mózhna dayékhat' na póyizdye?

Что вы производите?

Как вы оплачиваете
больничный лист?

Вы платите зарплату во время
декретного отпуска?

Женщины получают такую
же зарплату как и мужчины?

Сколько часов в день вы
работаете?

Вы не могли бы меня
сфотографировать?

Всё установлено.

Нажмите на кнопку и всё.

Можно я вас
сфотографирую?

Давайте сфотографируемся
вместе.

Я хочу сфотографироваться у
памятника Пушкину.

Улыбнитесь!

Где можно проявить и
напечатать фотографии?

Дайте, пожалуйста, ваш адрес
и я пришлю вам фотографии.

Вы тоже турист?

Откуда вы?

Тула интересный город для
туристов?

Туда можно доехать на
поезде?

How many hours does it take to get to . . . by train?	Skól'ka chisóf idyót póyist v . . . ?
How many days are you going to stay in Moscow?	Skól'ka dnyéy vy búditye vMaskvyé?
I want to go to Tula, if I have time.	Ya khachú payékhat' fTúlu, yésli u minýa búdyet vryémya.

What You May Hear

fatagrafíravat'	take pictures
putishéstvavat'	travel
inastrányets	foreigner
atkrýtka	postcard
pasylát'	send
sabirát'sa	gather
pámyatnik	monument
gósti	guests
uyezhát'	leave
priyezhát', pribyvát'	arrive
dabró pazhálavat'	welcome
turíst	tourist
vósyem' chisóf	eight o'clock
dyésyit' chisóf	ten o'clock
pastróyin vvasimnátsatam vyéke	built in eighteenth century
tsar'	tsar
zdániye	building
báshnya	tower
istóriya	history

Сколько часов идёт поезд в . . . ?

Сколько дней вы будете в
Москве?

Я хочу поехать в Тулу, если у
меня будет время.

фотографировать

путешествовать

иностранец

открытка

посылать

собираться

памятник

гости

уезжать

приезжать, прибывать

добро пожаловать

турист

восемь часов

десять часов

построен в восемнадцатом веке

царь

здание

башня

история

English-Russian Dictionary

Abbreviations used are: noun (n), verb (v),
adjective (adj), adverb (adv), masculine (m),
feminine (f) and plural (pl).

A

ability	sposóbnast'	способность
able	byt' fsastayánii	быть в состоянии
abroad	za granítsey	за границей
accept	prinimát'	принимать
accompany	sapravazhdát'	сопровождать
action	dyéystviye	действие
acting	dyéystvavat'	действовать
actor	aktyór	актёр
actress	aktrísa	актриса
actual	dyeystvítyel'ny	действительный
address	ádryes	адрес
adjust	prispasáblivatsa	приспосабливаться
administration	administrátsiya	администрация
admire	vaskhishchátsa	восхищаться
admission	priyóm	приём
adolescent	padróstak	подросток
adopt	usynavlyát',	усыновлять,
	prinimát'	принимать
adult	vzrosíly	взрослый
advance (v)	pradvigátsa,	продвигаться
(n)	pradvizhéniye	продвижение

adventure	priklyuchéniye	приключение
advice	savyét	совет
aeroplane	samalyót	самолёт
affect	dyéystvavat' na,	действовать на,
	parazhát'	поражать
afford	pazvalyát' sibyé	позволять себе
African	afrikánskiy	африканский
after	póslye	после
afternoon	ftaráya palavína dnya	вторая половина дня
in the afternoon	vaftaróy palavínye	во второй подовине
	dnya	дня
again	apyát'	опять
against	prótif	против
age	vózrast	возраст
agency	agyénstva	агентство
agree	saglashátsa	соглашаться
agriculture	syél'skaye	сельское
	khazyáystva	хозяйство
aim	tsel'	цель
air	vózdukh	воздух
air-mail	ávia-póchta	авиа–почта
alarm	trivóga	тревога
alike	byt pakhózhim,	быть похожим,
	adinákavy	одинаковый
alive	zhivóy	живой
all	vyes' (m)/fsya' (f)/	весь, вся, всё, все
	fsyó (n)/fsyé (pl)	
alley	piriúlak	переулок

allow	pazvalyát', razrishát'	позволять, разрешать
always	fsigdá	всегда
American	amyerikányets (m)/ amyerakánka (f)/ amyerakánskiy (adj)	американец/ американка/ американский
angry	sirdíty	сердитый
apartment	kvartíra	квартира
apple	yáblaka	яблоко
approximately	priblizítel'na	приблизительно
around *(surrounding)*	vakrúk	вокруг
arrive	pribyvát'	прибывать
art	iskústva	искусство
article *(newspaper)*	statiyá	статья
article *(item)*	pridmyét	предмет
ask	spráshivat', prasít'	спрашивать, просить
attend	prisútstvavat', pasishchát'	присутствовать посещать
attention	vnimániye	внимание
aunt	tyótya	тётя
awful	uzhásny	ужасный

B

back *(body part)*	spiná	спина
back *(direction)*	nazát	назад
bad	plakhóy	плохой
bag	súmka, mishók	сумка, мешок

baggage	bagázh	багаж
bakery	búlachnaya	булочная
ballet	balyét	балет
bandage	pavyázka, bint	повязка, бинт
bank	bank	банк
barber	parimákhyer	парикмахер
bargain	udáchnaya pakúpka	удачная покупка
basket	karzínka	корзинка
bath	vána	ванна
take a bath	prinyát' vánu	принять ванну
bathe	kupátsa	купаться
battery	bataryéya	батарея
beach	plyazh	пляж
bear (*animal*)	midvyét'	медведь
beautiful	krasívy	красивый
because	patamúshta	потому что
bed	kravát'	кровать
bedroom	spál'nya	спальня
beef	gavyádina	говядина
beer	píva	пиво
before	rán'she, pyéryit	раньше, перед
begin	nachinát'	начинать
behave	vistí sibyá	вести себя
believe	vyérit', palagát'	верить, полагать
beside	ryádam, ókala	рядом, около
best	lúchshiy	лучший
bicycle	vilasipyét	велосипед
birch tree	biryóza	берёза

bird	ptítsa	птица
black	chyórny	чёрный
blame	vinít'	винить
blanket	adiyála	одеяло
blood	krof'	кровь
blouse	blúzka	блузка
blue	galubóy	голубой
boat	lótka, súdna	лодка, судно
book	kníga	книга
bookcase	knízhny shkaf	книжный шкаф
booth	bútka, palátka	бутка, полатка
border	granítsa	граница
boring	skúchna	скучно
born	razhdyóny	рождённый
borrow	adálzhivat'	одалживать
boss	nachál'nik	начальник
bother	byespakóyit'	беспокоить
bottle	butýlka	бутылка
bowl	míska	миска
soup bowl	taryélka dlya súpa	тарелка для супа
box	yáshchik, karópka	ящик, коробка
boy	mál'chik	мальчик
brain	mozk	мозг
brake (v)	tarmazít'	тормозить
brake (n)	tórmaz	тормоз
brand	fabríchnaya márka, fírma	фабричная марка, фирма
bread	khlyep	хлеб

break (v)	lamát'	ломать
break (n)	pirirýv	перерыв
breakfast	záftrak	завтрак
breast	grut'	грудь
breathe	dyshát'	дышать
breath	dykhániye	дыхание
breeze	(lyókhkiy) vyétyer	(лёгкий) ветер
bribe	vzyátka	взятка
brief	krátkiy	краткий
bright	yárkiy	яркий
bring	prinasít'	приносить
British	anglichánin (m)/	англичанин/
	anglichánka (f)/	англичанка/
	anglískiy (adj)	английский
broadcast (v)	piridavát' pa rádio	передавать по
		радио
brother	brat	брат
brown	karíchnivy	коричневый
bruise	sinyák, ushýp	синяк, ушиб
budget	byudzhét	бюджет
build	stróyit'	строить
burn (v)	garyét'	гореть
burn (n)	zhar, azhók	жар, ожог
bus	aftóbus	автобус
bush	kust	куст
business	dyelá, bíznyes	дела, бизнес
busy	zányaty	занятый
butter	másla (slívachnaye)	масло (сливочное)

buy	pakupát', kupít'	покупать, купить

C

cab	taksí	такси
cabbage	kapústa	капуста
cable	kábyel	кабель
cake	pirók	пирог
calendar	kalindár'	календарь
call (v)	zvanít', zvat'	звонить, звать
calm	spakóyny	спокойный
camera	fotaaparát	фотоаппарат
camp	lágyer'	лагерь
can (to be able)	moch'	мочь
cancel	atminít'	отменить
cancer	rak	рак
candle	svichá	свеча
canoe	baydárka	байдарка
capable	spasóbny	способный
capital	stalítsa	столица
car	mashýna, aftamabíl'	машина, автомобиль
card (postal)	atkrýtka	открытка
card (business)	visítnaya kártachka	визитная карточка
card (credit)	kridítnaya kártachka	кредитная карточка
care	zabóta	забота
take care of	zabótitsa (a)	заботиться (о)
career	kar'yéra	карьера
careful	astarózhny	осторожный

carpet	kavyór	ковёр
carrot	markóf'	морковь
carry	nasít'	носить
case (*box*)	futlyár, yáshchik	футляр, ящик
cash (n)	nalíchnye dyén'gi	наличные деньги
ceiling	patalók	потолок
celebrate	práznavat'	праздновать
center	tsentr	центр
central	tsintrál'ny	центральный
certificate	udastaviryéniye	удостоверение
chair	stul	стул
chalk	myel	мел
chamber	paláta	палата
chance	shans	шанс
change (v)	minyát'	менять
chapter	glavá	глава
charity	blagatvarítyel'stva	благотворительство
chauffeur	shafyór	шофёр
cheap	dishóvy	дешёвый
cheat (*deceive*)	abmányvat'	обманывать
cheek	shcheká	щека
cheese	syr	сыр
chemical	khimícheskiy	химический
cherry	víshnya	вишня
chess	shákhmaty	шахматы
chicken	kúritsa	курица
child	ribyónok	ребёнок
chin	padbaródak	подбородок

china	farfór	фарфор
China	Kitáy	Китай
Chinese	kitáyets (m)/	китаец/китаянка/
	kitayánka (f)/	китайский
	kitáyskiy (adj)	
chocolate	shakalát	шоколад
choice	výbor	выбор
choose	vybirát'	выбирать
Christmas	razhdyestvó	рождество
church	tsérkaf'	церковь
cigarette	sigaryéta	сигарета
circle	kruk	круг
circus	tsyrk	цирк
citizen	grazhdanín (m)/	гражданин/
	grazhdánka (f)	гражданка
city	górat	город
civilization	tsivilizátsiya	цивилизация
clean (adj)	chísty	чистый
clear (adj)	yásny	ясный
clerk	slúzhashchiy	служащий
client	kliyént	клиент
climate	klímat	климат
climb (*ascend*)	padnimát'sa	подниматься
clock	chisý	часы
close	zakryvát'	закрывать
closet	shkaf	шкаф
clothes	adyézhda	одежда
cloud	óblaka	облака

club	klup	клуб
coach *(sports)*	tryénir	тренер
coast	pabiryézh'ye	побережье
coat	pal'tó	пальто
coffee	kófye	кофе
coincidence	safpadyéniye	совпадение
collect	sabirát'	собирать
colony	kalóniya	колония
comedy	kamyédiya	комедия
commerce	targóvlya	торговля
commercial (adj)	targóvy	торговый
commercial (n)	rekláma	реклама
common *(mutual)*	ópshchiy	общий
communication	kamunikátsiya	коммуникация
company	kampániya	компания
compare	srávnivat'	сравнивать
compete	saryevnavátsa	соревноваться
complain	zhálavat'sa	жаловаться
complete	zakánchivat'	заканчивать
complicate	uslazhnyát'	усложнять
composer	kampazítr	композитор
concentrate	sasridatóchitsa	сосредоточиться
concert	kantsért	концерт
conclude	zaklyuchát'	заключать
condition	uslóviye	условие
conference	kanfiryéntsiya	конференция
congratulate	pazdravlyát'	поздравлять

consider	shchitát', rassmátrivat'	считать, рассматривать
consist	sastayát'	состоять
contemporary	savrimyény	современный
contest	sarivnaśniye	соревнование
continue	pradalzhát'	продолжать
convenient	udóbny	удобный
conversation	razgavór	разговор
cool (adj)	prakhládny	прохладный
cooperate	satrúdnichat'	сотрудничать
coordinate	kaardiníravat'	координировать
copy (n)	kópiya	копия
copy (v)	snimát' kópiyu	снимать копию
correct (v)	ispravlyát'	исправлять
correctly	právil'na	правильно
cost (n)	tsiná	цена
cost (v)	stóit	стоит
cotton	khlópak	хлопок
couch	diván	диван
cough (n)	káshil'	кашель
cough (v)	káshlyat'	кашлять
country	straná	страна
cousin	dvayúradny brat (m)	двоюродный брат
cow	karóva	корова
craft (n)	rimisló	ремесло
crazy	sumashédshy	сумашедший
create	sazdavát'	создавать
crime	pryestuplyéniye	преступление

cry	krichát', plákat'	кричать, плакать
cucumber	aguryéts	огурец
culture	kul'túra	культура
cut (n)	paryés	порез
cut (v)	ryézat'	резать

D

dad	pápa	папа
daily	yezhidnyévny	ежедневный
dairy (*store*)	malóchny magazín	молочный магазин
damage (n)	ushchérp, ubýtki	ущерб, убытки
dance (n)	tányets	танец
dance (v)	tantsivát'	танцевать
danger	apásnast'	опасность
Danish	dátskiy	датский
dark	timnó	темно
darling	daragóy, míly	дорогой, милый
date (*time*)	chisló	число
daughter	doch'	дочь
day	dyen'	день
dead	myórtvy	мёртвый
deaf	glukhóy	глухой
dear	daragóy	дорогой
death	smyért'	смерть
deceive	abmányvat'	обманывать
decide	rishát'	решать
decision	rishéniye	решение
decorate	ukrashát'	украшать

deep	glubókiy	глубокий
degree *(temperature)*	grádus	градус
delicious	fkúsny, privaskhódny	вкусный, превосходный
demand (n)	tryébavaniye	требование
democracy	dimakrátiya	демократия
demonstrate	dimanstríravat'	демонстрировать
denial	atritsániye	отрицание
dental	zubnóy	зубной
deny	atritsát'	отрицать
depart	atpravlyátsa, uyezhát'	отправляться, уезжать
department	atdyél	отдел
depend	zavísyet'	зависеть
deposit (n)	vznos, fklad	взнос, вклад
depress	padavlyát'	подавлять,угнетать
describe	apísyvat'	описывать
desert	pustýnya	пустыня
deserve	zaslúzhivat'	заслуживать
design (n)	prayékt	проект
desire	zhilá010niye	желание
dessert	disyért	десерт
destruction	razrushéniye	разрушение
detail	padróbnast', ditál'	подробность, деталь
detergent	móyushiye sryédstva	моющие средства
determine	apridilyát'	определять
dial (v)	nabirát' nómir	набирать номер

diary	dnivník	дневник
dictionary	slavár'	словарь
differ	atlichátsa	отличаться
difficult	trúdny	трудный
digit, figure	tsýfra	цифра
dinner	abyéd	обед
direct	primóy	прямой
dirty	gryázny	грязный
disagree	ni saglashátsa	не соглашаться
disappear	ischizát'	изчезать
discuss	absuzhdát'	обсуждать
disease	balyézn'	болезнь
dish	blyúda, taryélka	бдюдо, тарелка
dismiss (from a	atpuskát', uval'nyát'	отпускать,
job)		увольнять
dive	nyryát'	нырять
divide	dyelít'	делить
divorce	razvód	развод
dog	sabáka	собака
doll	kúkla	кукла
door	dvyer'	дверь
double (adj)	dvaynóy	двойной
doubt (n)	samnyéniye	сомнение
downtown	tsentr górada	центр города
draft (n) (sketch)	nabrósak	набросок
draft (n) (in a room)	skvaznyák	сквозняк
drawing	risúnok	рисунок
drive	vadít' mashýnu	водить машину

dull	tupóy	тупой
dusk	súmyerki	сумерки
dust	pyl'	пыль
Dutch	galánskiy	голандский

E

each	kázhdy	каждый
eager	strimyáshchiysya	стремящийся
ear	úkha	ухо
earn	zarabátyvat'	зарабатывать
earth	zimlyá	земля
east	vastók	восток
Easter	páskha	пасха
easy	lyókhkiy	лёгкий
effect	dyéystviye,	действие,
	ryezul'tát	результат
efficient	ifiktívny	эфективный
egg	yitszó	яйцо
Egyptian	yegípitskiy	египетский
elbow	lókat'	локоть
elderly	stárshiy, pazhilóy	старший, пожилой
elect	vybirát'	выбирать
elephant	slon	слон
eleven	adínnatsat'	одиннадцать
elk	los'	лось
emancipate	emansipíravat'	эмансипировать
embarrass	smushchát'	смущать
embassy	pasól'stva	посольство

embrace	abnimát'	обнимать
emergency	kritíchiskaye palazhéniye	критическое положение
emotion	emótsiya	эмоция
employ *(hire)*	nanimát' na rabótu	нанимать на работу
empty	pustóy	пустой
enable	davát' vazmózhnast'	давать возможность
encourage	abadryát' paaschryát'	ободрять, поощрять
end	kanyéts	конец
endurance	tyerpyéniye, vynóslivast'	терпение, выносливость
engine	dvígatyel'	двигатель
engineer	inzhinyér	инжинер
English	anglíyskiy	английский
enhance	uluchshát'	улучшать
enjoy	paluchát' udavól'stviye	получать удовольствие
enlarge	uvilíchivat'	увеличивать
enough	dastátachna	достаточно
enrich	abagashchát'	обогащать
enter	fkhadít'	входить
enterprise	pryedpriyátiye	предприятие
entertain	razvlikát'	развлекать
enthusiasm	entuziázm	энтузиазм
entire	tsély, vyes'	целый, весь

to be entitled	imyét' práva	иметь право
entrance	fkhot	вход
envelope	kanvyeft	конверт
envious	zavíslivy	завистливый
equal	rávny	равный
era	éra	эра
error	ashýbka	ошибка
essay	sachinyéniye, essé	сочинение, эссэ
essential	sushchéstvyeny	существенный
estate	pamyést'ye	поместье
ethical	etíchny	этичный
European	yevrapyéyskiy	европейский
evade, avoid	izbyegát'	избегать
eve	kanún	канун
even *(numbered)*	chótny	чётный
evening	vyéchir	вечер
event	sabýtiye	событие
every	kázhdy	каждый
exact	tóchny	точный
exaggerate	priuvilíchivat'	преувеличивать
example	primyér	пример
exceed	privyshát'	превышать
excellent	privaskhódny	превосходный
except	krómye	кроме
excerpt	atrývak	отрывок
exchange (n)	abmyén	обмен
exclude	isklyuchát'	исключать
excuse (v)	izvinyát'	извинять

exercise (n)	uprazhnyéniye	упражнение
exhibit (n)	výstafka	выставка
expert	ekspyért	эксперт
expire	istyekát'	истекать
extend	pradlyevát'	продлевать

F

fabric	tkan'	ткань
face	litsó	лицо
fact	fakt	факт
factory	fábrika	фабрика
faculty, depart- ment *(of a university)*	fakul'tyét	факультет
fair	spravidlívy	справедливый
faith	vyéra	вера
fake	paddyélyvat'	подделывать
fall	pádat'	падать
family	syim'yá	семья
far	dalikó	далеко
farm	fyérma	ферма
fast	bístry	быстрый
fat	tólsty	толстый
father	atyéts	отец
father-in-law	svyóker	свёкр
February	fyevrál'	февраль
fear (v)	bayátsa	бояться
federal	fidiral'ny	федеральный

feel	chústvavat'	чувствовать
fence	zabór	забор
ferry	paróm	паром
festival	práznik	праздник
few	nimnóga	немного
field	pólye	поле
fight (n)	dráka	драка
figure (*numerical*)	tsyfra	цифра
figure (*physical*)	figúra	фигура
fill	napalnyát'	наполнять
film	plyónka (fota)	плёнка (фото)
finger	pályets	палец
fingernail	nógat'	ноготь
finish	kanchát'	кончать
Finn	fin (m)/fínka (f)	фин, финка
fire	agón'	огонь
firm	fírma	фирма
first	pyérvy	первый
fish (n)	rýba	рыба
fix	chinít'	чинить
flag	flak	флаг
flight	palyót	полёт
flower	tsvitók	цветок
fluent (*of speech*)	bégly	беглый
fly	litát'	летать
fog	tumán	туман
folk	narót	народ
follow	slyédavat'	следовать

foot	nagá	нога
force (n)	síla	сила
foreign	inastrány	иностранный
free	svabódny	свободный
freedom	svabóda	свобода
French	frantsúskiy	французский
friend	druk	друг
future	búdushchiye	будующее

G

gain	priabryetát'	приобретать
gallery	galiryéya	галерея
gamble	igrát' vazártnyye ígry	играть в азартные игры
game	igrá	игра
garage	garázh	гараж
garbage	músar	мусор
garden	sat	сад
garlic	chisnók	чеснок
gasoline	binzín	бензин
gate	varóta	ворота
gather	sabirát'	собирать
glass (*material*)	stikló	стекло
glass (*for drinking*)	stakán	стакан
general	ópshchiy	общий
generate	praizvadít'	производить
German	nyémyts (m)/	немец/немка/
	nyémka (f)/	немецкий
	nimyétskiy (adj)	

get *(receive)*	paluchát'	получать
gift	padárak	подарок
girl	dyévachka, dyévushka	девочка, девушка
give	davát'	давать
glad	rat (m)/rada (f)	рад/рада
glory	sláva	слава
go	ittí, khadít'	идти, ходить
goal	tsel'	цель
God	Bok	Бог
good	kharóshy, dóbry	хороший, добрый
governor	gubyernátar	губернатор
gown	vichyérniye plátiye	вечернее платье
graduate *(lit. to finish)*	zakánchivat'	заканчивать
grain	zirnó	зерно
grammar	gramátika	грамматика
grandfather	dyédushka	дедушка
grape	vinagrát	виноград
grass	travá	трава
grateful	blagadárny	благодарный
grave (n)	magíla	могила
gravy	padlífka	подливка
grease	zhyr	жир
great	vilikalyépniy	великолепный
Greek	gryek (m)/ grichánka (f)/ gryéchiskiy (adj)	грек/гречанка/ греческий

green	zelyóny	зелёный
ground	zimlyá	земля
groundwork	fundámyent, asnóva	фундамент, основа
grow	rastí	расти
guard	akhrána	охрана
guess	ugadát'	угодать
guilt	viná	вина
gun	reval'vyér, pistolyét	револьвер, пистолет
gusty	parývisty	порывистый
guy	páryen'	парень

H

habit	privýchka	привычка
hail	grat	град
hair	vólasy	волосы
half	palavína	половина
hello	zdrástvuytye	здравствуйте
hello (on telephone)	alyó	алло
ham	vyetchiná	ветчина
hammer	malatók	молоток
hand	ruká	рука
handle, pen	rúchka	ручка
handsome	krasívy	красивый
hang	vyéshat'	вешать
happen	sluchátsa	случаться
hard	tvyórdy	твёрдый
hardly	yedvá	едва

harm	vryet	вред
hat	shlyápa	шляпа
hate (v)	ninavídyet'	ненавидеть
have	imyét'	иметь
head	galavá	голова
headache	galavnáya bol'	головная боль
hear	slúshat'	слушать
heart	syértsye	сердце
heartburn	izzhóga	изжога
heat	zhará	жара
heel (bodypart)	pyátka	пятка
heel (of a shoe)	kablúk	каблук
height	vysatá	высота
heir	naslyédnik	наследник
help	pamagát'	помогать
here	zdyes'	здесь
hero	giróy	герой
hesitate	kalibátsa	колебаться
hi	privyét	привет
hide	pryátat'	прятать
high	visókiy	высокий
hill	kholm	холм
hint	namyók	намёк
hip	bidró	бедро
hire	nanimát'	нанимать
hit	udárit'	ударить
hold	dirzhát'	держать
hole	dyrá	дыра

holiday	práznik	праздник
home	dom	дом
homeland	ródina	родина
honest	chyésny	честный
honey	myot	мёд
honor	chyest'	честь
hook	kryuchók	крючок
hope	nadyézhda	надежда
horse	lóshat'	лошадь
hospitable	gastipriímny	гостеприимный
hospital	bal'nítsa	больница
host	khazyáin	хозяин
hot	garyáchiy	горячий
hotel	gastínitsa	гостиница
hour	chas	час
house	dom	дом
how/in what way	kak/kakím óbrazam	как/каким образом
hug	abnimát'	обнимать
huge	agrómny	огромный
human (adj)	chilavyéchiskiy	человеческий
humid (v)	vlázhny	влажный
humor	yúmar	юмор
hungry	galódny	голодный
hurry (v)	tarapít'sa	торопиться
hurt (v)	pavridít'	повредить
it hurts	balít	болит
husband	muzh	муж
husky (dog)	láyka (sabáka)	лайка (собака)

I

I	ya	я
ice	lyot	лёд
idea	idyéya	идея
if	yésli	если
ignore	ignaríravat'	игнорировать
ill	bal'nóy	больной
illiteracy	nigrámatnast'	неграмотность
illness	balyézn'	болезнь
imagine	vaabrazhát'	воображать
imitate	padrazhát', imitíravat'	подражать, имитировать
immature *(unripened)*	nizryély	незрелый
immerse	pagruzhát'	погружать
impact	vliyániye	влияние
impatience	nityerpyéniye	нетерпение
impeccable	byezupryéchny	безупречный
impolite	nivézhlivy	невежливый
importance	znachítilnast'	значительность
impress	fpichitlyát'	впечатлять
improve	uluchshát'	улучшать
incident	slúchay	случай
include	fklyuchát'	включать
income	dakhót	доход
increase (v)	uvilíchit'	увеличить
indicate	ukázyvat'	указывать
influence (n)	vliyániye	влияние

inform	saabshchát'	сообщать
insane	bezúmny	безумный
install	ustanávlivat'	устанавливать
insult (n)	askarblyéniye	оскорбление
insurance	strakhófka	страховка
introduce	pritstavlyát'	представлять
incest	fkládyvat'	вкладывать
iron (material)	zhilyéza	железо
island	óstraf	остров
Italian	italyányets (m)/	итальянец/
	italyánka (f)/	итальянка/
	italyanskiy (adj)	итальянский
itinerary	plan marshrúta,	план маршрута
	plan putishéstviya	план путешествия

J

jam (*preserves*)	dzhem	джем
jar	bánka	банка
jaw	chyélyust'	челюсть
jazz	dzhaz	джаз
jealous	rivnívy	ревнивый
job	rabóta	работа
journal (*diary*)	zhurnál, dnivník	журнал, дневник
judge	sud'ya	судья
juice	sok	сок
July	iyúl'	июль
jump	prýgat'	прыгать
June	iyún'	июнь

junior *(younger)*	mládshy	младший
junk	khlam	хлам
jury	prisyázhnye	присяжные
just (adv)	tól'ka shtó	только что
justice	pravasúdiye	правосудие
juvenile (n)	padróstak	подросток

K

keep	dyerzhát', sakhranyát'	держать, сохранять
kettle	cháynik	чайник
key	klyuch	ключ
kidnap	pakhishchát'	похищать
kidney	póchka	почка
kill	ubivát'	убивать
kind	dóbry	добрый
kindergarten	dyétskiy sat	детский сад
king	karól'	король
kitten	katyónak	котёнок
knee	kalyéna	колено
knife	nosh	нож
knock	stuchát'	стучать
know	znat'	знать
knowledge	znániye	знание

L

| label (n) | yarlýk | ярлык |
| laboratory | labaratóriya | лаборатория |

labor (n)	trut	труд
lack	nidastátak	недостаток
lacquer (n)	lak	лак
lacquer (adj)	lákiróvany	лакированный
lady	dáma	дама
lake	ózira	озеро
land (n)	zimlyá	земля
large	bal'shóy	большой
last, final	paslyédniy	последний
last, continue	pradalzhátsa	продолжаться
late	pózna, pózny	поздно, поздний
Latin	latínskiy	латинский
laugh (n)	smyekh	смех
lavatory	ubórnaya	уборная
lavender (adj)	lilóvy	лиловый
lawyer	yuríst, advakát	юрист, адвокат
lay, put	klast', palazhýt'	класть, положить
lead (v)	vistí, rukavadít'	вести, руководить
leader	vozht', rukavadítyel'	вождь, руководитель
leaf	list	лист
learn	uchítsa	учиться
leather	kózha	кожа
leave	uyezhát', ukhadít'	уезжать, уходить
lecture (n)	lyéktsiya	лекция
left (adj)	lyévy	левый
leg	nagá	нога
legal	yuridíchyeskiy, pravavóy	юридический, правовой

lemon	limón	лимон
lend	adalzhyvát'	отдолживать
length	dliná	длина
less	myén'she	меньше
lesson	urók	урок
lettuce	salát	салат
liberate	asvabazhdát'	освобождать
lid	krýshka	крышка
lie (n)	abmán	обман
lie (v)	abmánivat'	обманывать
live	zhizn'	жизнь
lift (v)	padnimát'	поднимать
light (n)	svyet	свет
light-weight	lyókhkiy	лёгкий
like (v)	nravitsa	нравится
like (adj)	pakhózhy	похожий
line	óchiryed'	очередь
lion	lyev	лев
lip	gubá	губа
liqueur	likyór	ликёр
listen	slúshat'	слушать
literature	litiratúra	литература
little	málin'kiy	маленький
live (v)	zhyt'	жить
lively	visyóly, azhivlyóny	весёлый, оживлённый
liver	pyéchin'	печень
loan (n)	zayóm	заём
loan (v)	davát' v zaymý	давать взаймы

local	mésny	местный
lock	zamók	замок
long	dlíny	длинный
look	smatryét'	смотреть
lose	tiryat'	терять
love (n)	lyubóf'	любовь
love (v)	lyubít'	любить
low	nískiy	низкий
luck	ydácha	удача
lunch	vtoróy zaftrak	второй завтрак

M

machine	mikhanízm, stanók	механизм, станок
madam	gaspazhá	госпожа
magazine	zhurnál	журнал
mail (n)	póchta	почта
main	glávny	главный
make	dyélat'	делать
male	muzhskóy	мужской
man	mushchína	мужчина
manage	upravlyát', spravlyátsa	управлять, справляться
manager	zavyédushchiy, rukavadítyel'	заведующий, руководитель
mankind	chilovyéchistva	человечество
mansion	asabnyák	особняк
many	mnóga	много
map	kárta	карта

March	mart	март
margarine	margarín	маргарин
marine	marskóy	морской
mark (n)	znak, métka	знак, метка
mark (v)	atmichát'	отмечать
market	rýnak	рынок
married	zhináty (m)/	женатый/замужем
	zámuzhim (f)	
marry	zhinítsa (m)/vikhadít	жениться/
	zámuzh (f)	выходить замуж
mathematics	matimátika	математика
matter	dyéla	дела
May	may	май
meal, food	yedá	еда
mean (v)	znáchit'	значить
measure (n)	myéra	мера
measure (v)	izmiryát'	измерять
medical	miditsýnskiy	медицинский
meet	vstryechát'	встречать
meeting	svidániye	свидание
memorize	zapaminát'	запоминать
mention (v)	upaminát'	упоминать
merchandise	taváry	товары
mess	byesparyádak	беспорядок
meter	shchyóchik	счётчик
middle	siridína	середина
milk	malakó	молоко
mineral water	minirál'naya vadá	минеральная вода

mirror	zyérkala	зеркало
miss, leave out	prapustít'	пропустить
mistake (n)	ashýbka	ошибка
modern	savrimyénny	современный
Monday	panidyél'nik	понедельник
money	dyén'gi	деньги
month	myésits	месяц
more	ból'she	больше
motel	matyél'	мотель
mother	mat', mama	мать, мама
mother-in-law	tyóshcha	тёща
motion	dvizhéniye	движение
mountain	gará	гора
mouth	rot	рот
move	dvígat'	двигать
much	mnóga	много
mushroom	grip	гриб
music	múzyka	музыка
mustard	garchítsa	горчица
mutual	vzaímny	взаимный

N

name	ímya	имя
napkin	salfyétka	салфетка
narrow	úzkiy	узкий
nasty	skvyérny, plakhóy	скверный, плохой
nation	nátsiya	нация
natural	yestyéstvinny	естественный

nature	priróda	природа
naval	vayéna-marskóy	военно–морской
navy	vayéna-marskóy flót	военно–морской флот
near	vblizí	вблизи
necessary	niabkhadímy	необходимый
neck	shyéya	щея
need (n)	nuzhdá	нужда
I need	mnyé núzhna	мне нужно
negotiate	vistí pirigavóry	вести переговоры
neighbor	sasyét	сосед
nephew	plimyánik	племянник
nerves	nyérvy	нервы
neutral	nitrál'ny	нейтральный
never	nikagdá	никогда
new	nóvy	новый
news	nóvasti	новости
next	slyédushchiy	следующий
nice	priyátny	приятный
night	noch'	ночь
no	nyet	нет
noise	shum	шум
noon	póldyen'	полдень
normal	narmálny	нормальный
north	syévir	север
nose	nos	нос
note (n)	zapíska	записка
nothing	nichivó	ничего

notice (v)	zamichát'	замечать
novel (n)	ramán	роман
November	nayábr'	ноябрь
now	sichás	сейчас
nude, naked	góly	голый
number	nómir	номер
nurse	myedsistrá	медсестра
nut	aryékh	орех

O

oath	klyátva	клятва
obey	slúshatsa	слушаться
object	pridmyét	предмет
object (v)	vazrazhát'	возражать
obligatory	abizátyelniy, niabkhadímy	обязательный, необходимый
obtain *(acquire)*	dabivát', priabritát'	добивать, приобретать
obvious	achivídny	очевидный
occasion	slúchiy	случай
ocean	akián	океан
October	aktyábr'	октябрь
odd	stránny	странный
offend	abizhát', askarblyát'	обижать, оскорблять
offer (v)	pridlagát'	предлагать
office	kabinyét, kantóra	кабинет, контора
officer	afitsyér	офицер

often	chásta	часто
ointment	mas'	мазь
old	stáry	старый
once	adín ras	один раз
onion	luk	лук
only	tól'ka	только
open (v)	atkrýt'	открыть
opera	ópira	опера
operator	apirátar	оператор
opinion	mnyéniye	мнение
oppose	byt' prótif	быть против
option (choice)	výbar	выбор
orange (n)	apil'sín	апельсин
orchard	fruktóvy sat	фруктовый сад
order (n)	paryádak	порядок
origin	praiskhazhdyéniye	происхождение
other	drugóy	другой
our	nash	наш
oval (adj)	avál'ny	овальный
own (adj)	svoy, sópstvyenny	свой, собственный

P

page	stranítsa	страница
pain	bol'	боль
paint (n)	kráska	краска
pair	pára	пара
pal (comrade)	tavárishch	товарищ
pale	blyédny	бледный

palm	ladón'	ладонь
pan	kastryúlya	кастрюля
pancakes	aládi, bliný	олади, блины
paper	bumága	бумага
parcel	pasýlka	посылка
parents	radítili	родители
park	park	парк
partake	prinimát' uchástiye	принимать участие
participant	uchásnik	участник
partner	partnyór	партнёр
passenger	pasazhýr	пассажир
past	próshlaye	прошлое
pay (v)	platít'	платить
payment	apláta	оплата
peace	mir	мир
peach	pyérsik	персик
peculiar	stránny	странный
pedagogical	pidagagíchiskiy	педагогический
pedestrian	pishikhót	пешеход
pen (*handle*)	rúchka	ручка
pencil	karandásh	карандаш
people	lyúdi	люди
pepper	pyérits	перец
perfect	prikrásny	прекрасный
performance	tiatrálnaye pridstavlyéniye	театральное представление
perfume	dukhí	духи
permission	razrishéniye	разрешение

permit (v)	razrishát'	разрешать
phone	tilifón	телефон
phoney	falshíviy	фальшивый
physician	vrach	врач
physicist	fízik	физик
piano	pianína	пианино
pick (*choose*)	sabirát', padbirát'	собирать,
		подбирать
pick up	padnimát'	поднимать
picture	kartína	картина
pig	svin'yá	свинья
pillow	padúshka	подушка
pilot	pilót	пилот
pink	rózavy	розовый
pitcher	kuvshýn	кувшин
place	myésta	место
plain	prastóy	простой
plane	samalyót	самолёт
plate	taryélka	тарелка
play (n)	p'yésa	пьеса
please	pazhálsta	пожалуйста
pleasure	udavól'stviye	удовольствие
plum	slíva	слива
pocket	karmán	карман
poet	payét	поэт
poison	yat, atráva	яд, отрава
police	palítsiya	полиция
police (*in Russia*)	milítsiya	милицля

polite	vyeźhlivy	вежливый
popular	papulyárny	популярный
prefer	pryedpachitát'	предпочитать
prepare	gatóvit', padgatóvit'	готовить,
		подготовить
prescribe	prapísyvat'	прописывать
(medicine)	(likárstva)	(лекарства)
prescription	retsépt	рецепт
pride	górdast'	гордость
principal	diryéktar shkóly	директор школы
prison	tyur'má	тюрьма
private	chásny, líchny	частный, личный
public (n)	públika,	публика,
	abschéstvenost'	общественность
public (adj)	publíchny	публичный

Q

quality	káchistva	качество
quarrel	sóra	ссора
quarter *(fraction)*	chyétvirt'	четверть
queen	karalyéva	королева
question	vaprós	вопрос
questionnaire	ankyéta, vaprósnik	анкета, вопросник
quickly	býstra	быстро
quiet	tíkhiy, spakóyny	тихий, спокойный
quit	brasát', astavlyát'	бросать, оставлять
quotation	tsytáta	цитата
quote (v)	tsytíravat'	цитировать

R

racial	rásavy	расовый
radio	rádio	радио
rage	gnyéf	гнев
rain	dózht'	дождь
rank	zvániye	звание
rapid	bystry	быстрый
rare	ryétkiy	редкий
rational	razúmny, ratsianál'ny	разумный, рациональный
raw	syróy	сырой
reach	dastavát', dastigát'	доставать, достигать
read (v)	chitát'	читать
ready	gatóvy	готовый
real	nastayáshchiy	настоящий
reason (*cause*)	prichína	причина
receipt	kvitántsiya	квитанция
recognize	uznavát', priznavát'	узнавать, признавать
recover	vyzdarávlivat'	выздоравливать
recreation	ótdykh, razvlichyéniye	отдых, развлечение
red	krásny	красный
reduce	uminshát'	уменьшать
refer	napravlyát', sylátsa	направлять, ссылаться
reflect	atrazhát'	отражать

reform	rifórma	реформа
refuse	atkázyvat'	отказывать
regard	uvazhéniye	уважение
region	óblast'	область
regular	rigulyárny	регулярный
rehearsal	ripitítsiya	репетиция
relax	raslablyátsa, atdykhát'	расслабляться, отдыхать
reliable	nadyózhny	надёжный
rely	palagátsa, davyeryát'	полагаться, доверять
remember	pómnit', fspaminát'	помнить, вспоминать
rent (n)	aryéndnaya pláta	арендная плата
rent (v)	brat' na prakát	брать на прокат
repair (n)	rimónt	ремонт
repair (v)	rimantíravat'	ремонтировать
repeat	paftaryát'	повторять
replace	zaminyát'	заменять
republic	rispúblika	республика
reside	prazhyvát'	проживать
respect (n)	uvazhéniye	уважение
respect (v)	uvazhát'	уважать
rest (n)	pakóy, ótdykh	покой, отдых
return (v)	vazvrashchátsa	возвращаться
revolver	rival'vyér	револьвер
right (*fair*)	právy, spravidlívy	правый, справедливый

ring	kal'tsó	кольцо
road	daróga	дорога
rock	kámin'	камень
roof	krýsha	крыша
room	kómnata	комната
round	krúgly	круглый
rude	grúby	грубый
run	byégat'	бегать

S

sad	pichal'ny	печальный
safe	bizapásny, nivridímy	безопасный, невредимый
sailor	matrós	матрос
salad	salát	салат
sale	pradázha	продажа
salt	sol'	соль
same	tót zhe	тот же
sample	abrazéts	образец
sand	pisók	песок
satisfy	udavlitvaryát'	удовлетворять
Saturday	subóta	суббота
sauce	sóus	соус
sausage	kalbasá	колбаса
save	spasát'	спасать
say	gavarít', skazát'	говорить, сказать
scar	shram	шрам
schedule	raspisániye	расписание

school	shkóla	школа
screen	ekrán, shýrma	экран, ширма
sea	mórye	море
seal *(official)* **(n)**	pichát'	печать
season	vryémya góda, sizón	время года, сезон
seat	myésta, sidyéniye	место, сидение
second	sikúnda	секунда
see *(look)*	vídit', smatryét'	видеть, смотреть
seek	iskát', razýskivat'	искать,
		разыскивать
seem	kazát'sa	казаться
it seems that . . .	kázhitsa, shto . . .	кажется, что . . .
select (v)	vybirát'	выбирать
send	pasylát'	посылать
senior (adj)	stárshy	старший
sentence	pridlazhéniye	предложение
September	sintyábr'	сентябрь
she	aná	она
shoot	stryelyát'	стрелять
shop (n)	magazín	магазин
short	karótkiy	короткий
shoulder	plichó	плечо
shy	rópkiy	робкий
sick	bal'nóy	больной
side	staraná	сторона
sign (n)	znak	знак
sign (v)	patpísyvat'	подписывать
simple	prastóy	простой

sit	sidyét'	сидеть
sky	nyéba	небо
sleep (v)	spat'	спать
slow	myédliny	медленный
small	málinkiy	маленький
snow (n)	snyék	снег
soon	skóra	скоро
speech	ryéch'	речь
stop (n)	astanófka	остановка
stop (v)	astanávlivatsa, prikrashchát'	останавливаться, прекращать
sugar	sákhar	сахар
Sunday	vaskrisyén'ye	воскресенье
swim	plávat'	плавать

T

table	stol	стол
take	brat', vzyát'	брать, взять
talk (v)	razgavárivat'	разговаривать
task	zadániye	задание
tax	nalók	налог
taxi	taksí	такси
tea	cháy	чай
teach	uchít'	учить
team	kamánda	команда
tenant	zhilyéts	жилец
term	srok	срок
theater	tiátr	театр

theory	tióriya	теория
thought	mysl'	мысль
thunder	grom	гром
Thursday	chitvérk	четверг
tiger	tigr	тигр
time	vryémya	время
tongue	yazýk	язык
tooth	zup	зуб
touch (v)	datrágivatsa	дотрагиваться
towel	palatyéntse	полотенце
trade	targóvlya	торговля
traffic	úlichnaye dvizhéniye, tránspart	уличное движение транспорт
train	póyist	поезд
travel (v)	putishéstvavat'	путешествовать
trip	putishéstviye, payéstka	путешествие, поездка
trouble	nipriyátnast'	неприятность
truck	gruzavík	грузовик
truth	právda	правда
Tuesday	ftórnik	вторник
tunnel	tunyél'	тунель
turn (v)	pavaráchivat'	поворачивать
twin	bliznyéts, dvayník	близнец, двойник
type (n)	tip, abrazyéts	тип, образец
type (v)	picháta'	печатать

U

ugly	uródlivy, nikrasívy	уродливый, некрасивый
uncle	dyádya	дядя
underline	padchyórkivat'	подчёркивать
uniform	forma	форма
unite	´saidinyátsa	соединяться
upset (v)	rastráivat'	растраивать
upstairs	navirkhú	наверху
usage	upatriblyéniye	употребление
use (v)	upatriblát', priminyát'	употреблять, применять
usual	abýchny	обычный

V

vacancy	vakánsiya	вакансия
valid	dyeystvítil'ny	действительный
value	tsennost'	ценность
variety	raznaabráziye	разнообразие
village	diryévnya	деревня
vineyard	vinagrádnik	виноградник
visa	víza	виза
vitamin	vitamín	витамин
vacation	ótpusk	отпуск
volume (book)	tom	том
vote (v)	galasavát'	голосовать
voyage	marskóye putishéstviye	морское путешествие

vulgar	grúby, vul'gárny	грубый, вульгарный

W

wait (v)	zhdat'	ждать
waiter	afitsiántka (f)/ afitsiánt (m)	официантка/ официант
wake *(awake)*	prasipátsa, budít'	просыпаться, будить
wall	stená	стена
wander	bradít'	бродить
want	khatyét'	хотеть
war	vayná	война
warm	tyóply	тёплый
wash	myt'	мыть
watch (v)	nablyudát', slidít'	наблюдать, следить
water	vadá	вода
wave (n) *(ocean)*	valná	волна
way	daróga, put'	дорога, путь
weak	sláby	слабый
wear	nacít'	носить
weather	pagóda	погода
Wednesday	sryedá	среда
week	nidyélya	неделя
weigh	vzvyéshivat'	взвешивать
welcome	dabró pazhálavat'	добро пожаловать
well	kharashó	хорошо
west	západ	запад
wet	mokry	мокрый

what	shto	что
when	kagdá	когда
which	kakóy	какой
who	kto	кто
whole	tsély	целый
wide	shirókiy	широкий
wild	díkiy	дикий
win	vyígrivat', pabizhdát'	выигрывать, побеждать
wind (n)	vyétir	ветер
window	aknó	окно
wine	vinó	вино
wish (n)	zhilániye	желание
wolf	volk	волк
woman	zhénshchina	женщина
word	slóva	слово
work (n)	rabóta	работа
world	mir, svyét	мир, свет
wound	rána	рана
write	pisát'	писать
wrong	niprávil'ny	неправильный

X

| X-ray | ryentgyén | рентген |

Y

| yacht | yákhta | яхта |
| yard | dvor | двор |

year	got	год
yellow	zhólty	жёлтый
yes	da	да
yesterday	vchirá	вчера
young	maladóy	молодой

Z

zero	nul'	нуль
zoo	zaapárk	зоопарк
zoology	zaalógiya	зоология

РУССКО–АНГЛИЙСКИЙ СЛОВАРЬ

А

август	August	ávgust
авиация	aviation	aviátsia
автор	author	ávtar
администратор	administrator	administrátar
актёр	actor	aktyór
актри́са	actress	aktriśa
акционер	stockholder	aktsianyér
американец	American	amyerikányets
ананас	pineapple	ananás
аптека	drug store	aptyéka
арбуз	watermelon	arbús
ароматический	aromatic	aramatícheskiy
архив	archives	arkhíf
архитектура	architecture	arkhityektúra
ассоциация	association	asatsiátsiya

Б

бабушка	grandmother	bábushka
багаж	luggage	bagásh
базар	market	bazár
бакалея	grocery	bakalyéya
бандит	bandit	bandít'
банк	bank	bank

баскетбол	basketball	baskitból
бассеий	swimming pool	basyéyn
бегать	run	byégat'
белый	white	byély
бензин	gasoline	binzín
беседа	conversation	bisyéda
беспокоить	disturb	byespakóit'
бесчувственный	insensitive	byeschústvyenny
библиотека	library	bibliatyéka
билет	ticket	bilyét
благодарить	thank	blagadarít'
блеснуть	shine	blyesnút'
боль	pain	bol'
борода	beard	baradá
борщ	borscht	borshch
брак	marriage	brak
брат	brother	brat
брать	take	brat'
бронировать	reserve	braníravat'
будить	wake	budít'
будущий	future	búdushchiy
бумага	paper	bumága
бутылка	bottle	butýlka
быть	be	byt'

В

| валюта | foreign currency | valyúta |
| ванна | bath | vána |

ваш	your	vash
вверх	up	vvyerkh
вечер	evening	vyéchyer
вдоль	along	vdol'
вдруг	suddenly	vdruk
век	century	vyek
велосипед	bicycle	vilasipyét
вершина	top, summit	vyershýna
вес	weight	vyes
весна	spring (season)	vyesná
вести	lead	vistí
весы	scales	vyesý
ветер	wind	vyétyer
ветка	branch	vyétka
видеть	see	vídit'
вина	guilt	viná
вино	wine	vinó
висеть	hang	visyét'
вишня	cherry	víshnya
включить	turn on	fklyuchít'
вместо	instead of	vmyésta
вода	water	vadá
водитель	driver	vadityel'
возврат	return (n)	vazvrát
воздух	air	vózdukh
война	war	vayná
волна	wave	valná
восток	east	vastók

| восход | rising | vaskhót |
| высота | height | vysatá |

Г

газ	gas	gas
галстук	tie	gálstuk
гастроном	grocery store	gastranóm
гитара	guitar	gitára
глава	chapter	glavá
главный	main	glávny
глаз	eye	glas
глина	clay	glína
глубокий	deep	glubókiy
глупый	stupid	glúpy
глядеть	look (v)	glidyét'
год	year	got
голос	voice	gólas
голосовать	vote	galasavát'
голубой	blue	galubóy
голый	naked	góly
гора	mountain	gará
гореть	burn	garyét'
гостиница	hotel	gastínitsa
готовить	cook (v)	gatóvit'
гриб	mushroom	grip
громкий	loud	grómkiy
грузин	Georgian	gruzín
грунт	soil	grunt

| группа | group | grúpa |
| густой | thick | gustóy |

Д

да	yes	da
дама	lady	dáma
дать	give	dat'
двигатель	engine	dvígatyel'
девочка	girl	dyévachka
действительно	indeed	dyestvítyel'na
декан	dean	dyekán
демократ	democrat	dimakrát
день	day	dyen'
деньги	money	dyén'gi
деталь	detail	dyetál
дирижёр	conductor	dirizhór
диск	disk	disk
длина	length	dliná
добрый	kind	dóbry
довольно	enough	davól'na
договор	agreement	dagavór
должен	must	dólzhin
дольше	longer	dól'she
дополнение	addition	dapalnyéniye
дорогой	dear	daragóy
доска	board	daská
дочь	daughter	doch
драма	drama	dráma

друг	friend	druk
думать	think	dúmat'
дурак	fool (n)	durák
дым	smoke	dym
дюжина	dozen	dyúzhina

Е

едва	barely	yedvá
ёлка (новогодняя)	Christmas tree	yólka (navagódnyaya)
если	if	yésli
естественный	natural	yestyéstvyenny
ещё	still, yet, more	yishchó

Ж

жакет	jacket	zhakyét
жара	heat	zhará
жаргон	slang	zhargón
жареный	fried	zháryeny
жевательный	chewing	zhivátyel'ny
железо	iron	zhilyéza
жёлтый	yellow	zhólty
жемчуг	pearl	zhémchuk
жена	wife	zhiná
жениться	marry	zhinítsa
живописный	picturesque	zhivapísny
жир	fat (n)	zhyr
журнал	magazine	zhurnál

З

за	behind	za
забывать	forget	zabyvát'
завещание	will (n)	zavishchániye
завод	factory	zavót
загород	suburb	zágarat
заказать	order (v)	zakazát'
закат	sunset	zakát
закон	law	zakón
закрыть	close (v)	zakrýt'
закурить	smoke (v)	zakurít'
зал	hall	zal
залив	bay	zalíf
замечание	note (n)	zamichániye
запад	west	zápat
зарплата	salary	zarpláta
зарубежный	foreign	zarubyézhny
заслуга	merit	zaslúga
защита	defense	zashchíta
звук	sound	zvuk
здание	building	zdániye
земля	earth	zimlyá
зеркало	mirror	zyérkala
знак	sign	znak
значить	mean	znáchit'
золото	gold	zólata
зонт	umbrella	zont
зрение	eyesight	zryéniye

| зуб | tooth | zup |
| зять | son-in-law | zyat' |

И

игла	needle	iglá
играть	play (v)	igrát'
идти	go	ití
избиратель	voter	izbiratyel'
известия	news	izvyéstiya
изменить	change (v)	izminít'
изобретать	invent	izabritát'
изумительный	amazing	izumítyel'ny
изумруд	emerald	izumrút
икона	icon	ikóna
имя	name	ímya
индеец	Indian	indyéyits
инженер	engineer	inzhinyér
инфляция	inflation	inflyátsiya
искать	seek	iskát'
искра	spark	iskrá
исследование	research	islyédavaniye
историк	historian	istórik

К

кабина	cabin (for vehicles)	kabína
казаться	seem	kazátsa
как	how	kak
каменистый	rocky	kamyenísty

канал	canal	kanál
кастрюля	saucepan	kastryúlya
катер	boat	kátyer
квартира	apartment	kvartíra
кино	movies	kinó
киоск	kiosk, newstand	kiósk
кислород	oxygen	kislarót
кладбище	cemetery	kládbishchye
класс	class	klas
ключ	key	klyuch
кожа	skin	kózha
колбаса	sausage	kalbasá
колено	knee	kalyéna
командовать	command (v)	kamándavat'
конец	end (n)	kanyéts
контракт	contract	kantrákt
корова	cow	karóva
король	king	karól'
королева	queen	karalyéva
корона	crown	karóna
кот	cat (m)	kot
кофе	coffee	kófye
кошка	cat (f)	kóshka
красный	red	krásny
крест	cross	kryest
крик	cry (n)	krik
кровь	blood	krof'
кроме	besides	krómye

круглый	round	krúgly
культура	culture	kul'túra
купаться	swim, bathe	kupátsa
курорт	resort	kurórt

Л

лёгкий	light (adj)	lyókhkiy
лёд	ice	lyot
лежать	lie, down (v)	lyezhát'
ленивый	lazy	linívy
лес	forest	lyes
летать	fly	lyetát'
лето	summer	lyéta
лечить	treat	lichít'
лидер	leader	lídyer
ликёр	liqueur	likyór
лимон	lemon	limón
лопата	shovel (n)	lapáta
лук	onion	luk
лучше	better	lúchshe
лев	lion	lyef
любить	love (v)	lyubít'
люди	people	lyúdi

М

магазин	store	magazín
маленький	small	málin'kiy
маска	mask	máska

мать	mother	mat'
машина	car	mashýna
мебель	furniture	myébyel'
месяц	month	myésyits
металл	metal	myetáll
метель	snowstorm	mityél'
минимальный	minimum	minimál'ny
мнение	opinion	mnyéniye
много	many	mnóga
могила	grave	magíla
мой	my	moy
молиться	pray	malítsa
молодёжь	young people	maladyósh
молоко	milk	malakó
монета	coin	manyéta
море	sea	mórye
мороженое	ice cream	marózhinaye
моряк	sailor	maryák
мост	bridge	most
мужчина	man	mushchína
мыть	wash	myt'
мягкий	soft	myákhkiy

Н

награда	reward	nagráda
надежда	hope (n)	nadyézhda
найти	find (v)	naytí
налево	to the left	nalyéva

направо	to the right	napráva
население	population	nasilyéniye
начало	beginning	nachála
небо	sky	nyéba
неизвестный	unknown	nyeizvyésny
ненавидеть	hate (v)	nyenavidyit'
несколько	several	nyéskol'ka
нести	carry	nistí
нефть	oil	nyeft'
низкий	low	nískiy
новости	news	nóvasti
нос	nose	nos
ночь	night	noch'
нужда	need (n)	nuzhdá

О

оба	both	óba
обаятельный	charming	abayátyel'ny
обвинять	blame (v)	abvinyát'
обед	dinner	abyét
обезьяна	monkey	abyez'yána
обеспечивать	provide	abyespyéchivat'
обида	offense	abída
область	region	óblast'
обнаружить	find	abnarúzhit'
образованный	educated	abrazóvanny
общий	common	ópshchiy
обычай	tradition	abýchiy

огромный	huge	agrómny
огурец	cucumber	aguryéts
одежда	clothes	adyézhda
однако	however	adnáka
оклад	salary	aklát
округ	region	ókruk
он	he	on
опять	again	apyát'
оранжевый	orange (adj)	aránzhivy
оскорбить	insult (v)	askarbít'
основа	base	asnóva
ответить	answer (v)	atvyétit'
ответственность	responsibility	atvyétstvyennast'
отец	father	atyéts
откровенный	frank	atkravyénny
открывать	open (v)	atkryvát'
отпуск	vacation	ótpusk
отчётливый	distinct	atchyótlivy
офицер	officer	afitsyér
официальный	official	afitsiál'ny
официант	waiter	afitsiánt
охота	hunting	akhóta
оценивать	estimate (v)	atsyénivat'
очищать	clean (v)	achishchát'
очки	glasses	achkí
ошибаться	make a mistake	ashybátsa

П

падать	fall	pádat'
папироса	cigarette *(Russian style)*	papirósa
парк	park	park
пар	steam	par
партия	political party	pártiya
парус	sail	párus
передний	front	piryédniy
перейти	cross (v)	piryeití
перекусить	have a snack	pirikusít'
перелом	break (n)	pirilóm
переменить	change (v)	pirimyenít'
перерыв	pause *(break)* (n)	pirirýv
пересадить	transplant	pirisadít'
перестроить	rebuild	piristróit'
перец	pepper	pýerits
петрушка	parsley	pitrúshka
петь	sing	pyet'
печень	liver	pyéchyin'
пианино	piano	pianína
пиво	beer	píva
пирог	pie	pirók
пистолет	gun	pistalyét
плод	fruit	plot
плохой	bad	plakhóy
плясать	dance (v)	plyisát'
повар	cook (n)	póvar

повернуть	turn (v)	pavyernút'
подобный	similar	padóbny
подогреть	warm up	padagrýet'
поезд	train	póyist
покупатель	customer	pakupátyel'
положение	situation	palazhéniye
поломаться	break, get broken	palamátsa
получать	get	paluchát'
помогать	help (v)	pamagát'
понятие	concept	panyátiye
пористый	porous	póristy
посередине	in the middle	pasryedínye
поток	flow	patók
потолок	ceiling	patalók
похвала	praise (n)	pakhvalá
почта	mail *(post office)*	póchta
почти	almost	pachtí
поэзия	poetry	paéziya
правда	truth	právda
правило	rule	právila
президент	president	prizidyént
преподавать	teach	pryepadavát'
пригород	suburb	prígarat
приём	reception	priyóm
прийти	come	priytí
пример	example	primyér
приправа	seasoning	pripráva
природа	nature	priróda

провод	wire	próvat
промышленность	industry	pramýshlyenast'
против	against	prótif
прямой	straight	primóy
прятать	hide	pryátat'
публика	public	públika
пшеница	wheat	pshinítsa
пыль	dust	pyl'
пятно	stain	pitnó

Р

работа	job	rabóta
радио	radio	rádio
разбить	break (v)	razbít'
развить	develop	razvít'
разгружать	unload	razgruzhát'
разрешать	permit, allow	razrishát'
рана	wound (n)	rána
расписание	schedule (n)	raspisániye
ребята	children	ribyáta
ревность	jealousy	ryévnast'
регулировать	regulate	rigulíravat'
редкий	rare	ryétkiy
резать	cut (v)	ryézat'
результат	result	ryezul'tát
рейс	flight	ryeys
река	river	ryeká
реклама	advertising	rikláma

рекомендовать	recommend	rikamindaváť
религия	religion	rilígiya
ремонтировать	repair	rimantíravať
речь	speech	ryech'
рис	rice	ris
рука	hand	ruká
руководить	manage, supervise	rukavadíť
ручка	pen	rúchka
рыба	fish	rýba
рынок	market	rýnak

С

салат	salad	salát
сам, сама	myself	sam (m), samá (f)
сапоги	boots	sapagí
свадьба	wedding	svád'ba
свежий	fresh	svyézhy
свёкла	beet	svyókla
свёкор	father-in-law	svyókar
свекровь	mother-in-law	svyekróf'
свет	light (n)	svyét
свобода	freedom	svabóda
север	north	syévir
седой	gray (hair)	syedóy
сейчас	now	sichás
секрет	secret	sikryét
секунда	second (n)	sikúnda
селёдка	herring	silyótka

семья	family	sim'yá
сёмга	salmon	syómga
серебро	silver (n)	siryebró
серьги	earrings	syér'gi
сестра	sister	sistrá
сесть	sit down	syést'
сила	strength	síla
симфония	symphony	simfóniya
сколько	how much	skól'ka
скучный	boring	skúshny
слава	glory	sláva
смех	laugh (n)	smyekh
совет	advice	savyét
сотрудник	employee	satrúdnik
спать	sleep (v)	spat'
спектакль	performance	spyektákl'
спина	back (n)	spiná
спрос	demand	spros
стадион	stadium	stadión
статуя	statue	státuya
стеклянный	made of glass	stiklyánny
стена	wall	styená
стереть	wipe off	stiryét'
стол	table	stol
строить	build	stróit'
студент	student (m)	studyént
студентка	student (f)	studyéntka
суп	soup	sup

Т

таблица	table *(chart)*	tablítsa
так	so	tak
такси	taxi	taksí
тащить	pull	´tashchít'
твёрдый	hard, firm	tvyórdy
театр	theater	tiátr
терять	lose	tiryát'
тётя	aunt	tyótya
трава	grass	travá
транспорт	transport	tránsport
троллейбус	trolleybus	tralyéybus
тропический	tropical	trapíchyeskiy
тротуар	sidewalk	tratuár
труд	labor	trut
туфли	shoes	túfli
тяжёлый	heavy	tizhóly

У

уважать	respect	uvazhát'
уда́р	blow (n)	udár
ударение	stress *(syllabic)*	udaryéniye
уйти	leave	uytí
умереть	die	umiryét'
умный	clever	úmny
универмаг	department store	univyermák
университет	university	univyersityét
усы	mustache	usý

утро	morning	útra
ученик	pupil	uchiník
учитель	teacher	uchítyel'
учить	teach, learn	uchít'

Ф

фабрика	factory	fábrika
факт	fact	fakt
ферма	farm	fyérma
фигура	figure	figúra
физика	physics	fízika
фильм	movie	fil'm
фонд	fund	font
фотография	photography, photograph	fatagráfiya
фундамент	foundation	fundámyent
фут	foot (measure)	fut

Х

характер	character	kharáktyer
хвастать	brag	khvástat'
химия	chemistry	khímiya
хлеб	bread	khlyep
хлопать	applaud	khlópat'
хлопок	cotton	khlópak
ходить	walk (v)	khadít'
холодный	cold (adj)	khalódny
хороший	good	kharóshy

| хотеть | want | khatyét' |
| хрупкий | fragile | khrúpkiy |

Ц

цветной	color (adj)	tsvyetnóy
цветок	flower	tsvitók
цель	target *(goal)*	tsel'
цена	price	tsiná
церковь	church	tsérkaf'
цифра	number	tsýfra
цыплёнок	chicken	tsiplyónak

Ч

чай	tea	chay
час	hour	chas
часто	often	chásta
часы	watch	chisý
чашка	cup	chyáshka
чек	check	chyek
человек	person	chilavyék
чёрный	black	chyórny
читать	read	chitát'
что	what	shto
чувствовать	feel	chústvavat'

Ш

| шаг | step | shak |
| шар | balloon | shar |

шахматы	chess	shákhmaty
шахта	mine *(shaft)*	shákhta
шина	tire	shýna
широкий	wide	shirókiy
школа	school	shkóla
школьник	student	shkól'nik
шоколад	chocolate	shakalát
шоссе	road	shosé
шум	noise	shum
шутить	joke (v)	shutít'
шутка	joke (n)	shútka

Щ

щедрость	generosity	shchyédrast'
щи	cabbage soup	shchi
щиколотка	ankle	shchíkalatka

Э

экзамен	test	egzámyen
экземпляр	example	egzimplyár
экипаж	crew	ekipásh
экран	screen	ekrán
эксперт	expert	ekspyért
эмигрант	emigrant	emigránt
эра	era	éra
это	this, this is	éta

Ю

юг	south	yuk
ювелир	jeweler	yuvilír
юмор	humor	yúmar
юность	youth *(adolescence)*	yúnast'
юрист	lawyer	yuríst

Я

яблоко	apple	yáblaka
явление	phenomenon	yivlyéniye
язык	language *(tongue)*	yizýk
яйцо	egg	yiytsó
яркий	bright	yárkiy
ясно	clearly	yásna
ящик	box	yáshchik

Appendix

Weekdays

Monday	panidyél'nik	понедельник
Tuesday	ftórnik	вторник
Wednesday	sryedá	среда
Thursday	chitvyérk	четверг
Friday	pyátnitsa	пятница
Saturday	subóta	суббота
Sunday	vaskrisyen'ye	воскресенье

(The week in Russia begins on Monday)

Months

January	yinvár'	январь
February	fivrál'	февраль
March	mart	март
April	apryel'	апрель
May	may	май
June	iyún'	июнь
July	iyúl'	июль
August	ávgust	август
September	sintyábr'	сентябрь
October	aktyábr'	октябрь
November	nayábr'	ноябрь
December	dikábr'	декабрь

Seasons

winter	zimá	зима
spring	visná	весна
summer	lyéta	лето
fall	ósin'	осень

Colors

red	krásny	красный
lightblue, dark blue	galubóy, síniy	голубой, синий
black	chórny	чёрный
white	byély	белый
brown	karíchnyevy	коричневый
green	zilyóny	зелёный
yellow	zhólty	жёлтый
gray	syéry	серый

Numbers

0	nul'	нуль
1	adín	один
2	dva	два
3	tri	три
4	chitýri	четыре
5	pyat'	пять
6	shest'	шесть
7	syem'	семь
8	vósyem'	восемь
9	dyévyit'	девять
10	dyésyit'	десять

20	dvátsat'	двадцать
30	trítsat'	тридцать
40	sórak	сорок
50	pidisyát	пятьдесят
60	shisdisyát	шестьдесят
70	syém'disit	семьдесят
80	vósim'disit	восемьдесят
90	divinósta	девяносто
100	sto	сто

Ordinal Numbers

first	pyérvy	первый
second	ftaróy	второй
third	tryétiy	третий
fourth	chitvyórty	четвёртый
fifth	pyáty	пятый
sixth	shistóy	шестой
seventh	sid'móy	седьмой
eighth	vas'móy	восьмой
ninth	divyáty	девятый
tenth	disyáty	десятый

Time

What time is it?	Skól'ka vryémini?	Сколько времени?
		Который час?
1:00 P.M.	chas dnya	час дня
2:00 A.M.	dva chisá nochi	два часа ночи
10:00 A.M.	dyésyit' chisóf utrá	десять часов утра

4:30 P.M.	palavína pyátava	половина пятого
8:45 A.M.	byes pitnátsati	без пятнадцати
	dyévit', byes	девять, без
	chetvirti dyévit'	четверти девять
9:10 A.M.	dyésit' minút	десять минут
	disyátava	десятого

Weights and Measures
Linear Measure

1 mile = 1,760 yards = 5,280 feet = 1,609 kilometers

1 yard = 3 feet = 91.44 centimeters

1 foot = 12 inches = 30.48 centimeters

1 inch = 2.54 centimeters

Square Measure

1 square mile = 640 (American) acres = 258.999 hectares

1 acre = 43.6 square feet = 4.8 square yards = 0.405 hectares

1 square yard = 9 square feet = 0.836 square meters

1 square foot = 144 square inches = 929 square centimeters

1 square inch = 6.45 square centimeters

Weight Measure

1 ton = 1.016 metric tons

1 pound = 16 ounces = 453.592 grams

1 ounce = 28.350 grams

Liquid Measure

1 gallon = 4 quarts = 8 pints = 3.785 liters

1 quart = 2 pints = 0.946 liters

1 pint = 2 cups = 0.47 liters

1 cup = 0.285 liters

Temperature

Fahrenheit - F	Centigrade - C
-40	-40
32	0
40	4.4
50	10.0
60	15.6
70	21.1
80	26.7
90	32.2
100	37.8

Comparative Clothing Sizes

Ladies - Dresses, Suits		Ladies - Shoes	
Russian	American	Russian	American
40	10	36	6
42	12	37	7
44	14	38	8
46	16	40	9
48	18		
50	20		

Gentlemen - *Suites, Overcoats*		*Gentlemen -* *Shoes*	
Russian	*American*	*Russian*	*American*
46	36	41	8
48	38	42	9
50	40	43	10
52	42	44	11
54	44	45	12
56	46		

FOREIGN LANGUAGE BOOKS

Multilingual
The Insult Dictionary:
  How to Give 'Em Hell in 5 Nasty
  Languages
The Lover's Dictionary:
  How to be Amorous in 5 Delectable
  Languages
Multilingual Phrase Book
Let's Drive Europe Phrasebook
CD-ROM "Languages of the World":
  Multilingual Dictionary Database

Spanish
Vox Spanish and English Dictionaries
NTC's Dictionary of Spanish False Cognates
Nice 'n Easy Spanish Grammar
Spanish Verbs and Essentials of Grammar
Getting Started in Spanish
Spanish à la Cartoon
Guide to Spanish Idioms
Guide to Correspondence in Spanish
The Hispanic Way

French
NTC's New College French and English
  Dictionary
French Verbs and Essentials of Grammar
Real French
Getting Started in French
Guide to French Idioms
Guide to Correspondence in French
French à la Cartoon
Nice 'n Easy French Grammar
NTC's Dictionary of *Faux Amis*
NTC's Dictionary of Canadian French
Au courant: Expressions for Communicating in
  Everyday French

German
Schöffler-Weis German and English Dictionary
Klett German and English Dictionary
Getting Started in German
German Verbs and Essentials of Grammar
Guide to German Idioms
Street-wise German
Nice 'n Easy German Grammar
German à la Cartoon
NTC's Dictionary of German False Cognates

Italian
Zanichelli Super-Mini Italian and English
  Dictionary
Zanichelli New College Italian and English
  Dictionary
Getting Started in Italian
Italian Verbs and Essentials of Grammar

Greek
NTC's New College Greek and English
  Dictionary

Latin
Essentials of Latin Grammar

Hebrew
Everyday Hebrew

Chinese
Easy Chinese Phrasebook and Dictionary

Korean
Korean in Plain English

Polish
The Wiedza Powszechna Compact Polish and
  English Dictionary

Swedish
Swedish Verbs and Essentials of Grammar

Russian
Complete Handbook of Russian Verbs
Essentials of Russian Grammar
Business Russian
Basic Structure Practice in Russian

Japanese
Easy Kana Workbook
Easy Hiragana
Easy Katakana
101 Japanese Idioms
Japanese in Plain English
Everyday Japanese
Japanese for Children
Japanese Cultural Encounters
Nissan's Business Japanese

"Just Enough" Phrase Books
Chinese, Dutch, French, German, Greek,
  Hebrew, Hungarian, Italian, Japanese,
  Portuguese, Russian, Scandinavian,
  Serbo-Croat, Spanish
Business French, Business German, Business
  Spanish

Audio and Video Language Programs
Just Listen 'n Learn Spanish, French,
  German, Italian, Greek, and Arabic
Just Listen 'n Learn...Spanish,
  French, German PLUS
Conversational...Spanish, French, German,
  Italian, Russian, Greek, Japanese, Thai,
  Portuguese in 7 Days
Practice & Improve Your...Spanish, French,
  Italian, and German
Practice & Improve Your...Spanish, French,
  Italian, and German PLUS
Improve Your...Spanish, French, Italian, and
  German: The P&I Method
VideoPassport French
VideoPassport Spanish
How to Pronounce...Spanish, French,
  German, Italian, Russian, Japanese
  Correctly

PASSPORT BOOKS
a division of *NTC Publishing Group*
Lincolnwood, Illinois USA